KU-407-983

Praise for Phyllis Curott and Spells for Living Well

"Spells for Living Well is a refreshingly clear book that is a joy to read and full of creative insights. If the idea of 'casting spells' is new to you, this book will open your eyes to the potential of the magical art to change our lives for the better. If you are an experienced witch, Phyllis Curott's wisdom will help you reflect on and deepen your personal practice."

VIVIANNE CROWLEY, PH.D., HIGH PRIESTESS OF
WICCA AND AUTHOR OF *WILD ONCE*

"Phyllis Curott walks her talk and lives her craft—all that she does is aligned with the highest integrity and light. It's teachers like Phyllis that make the world a brighter place!"

KYLE GRAY, BEST-SELLING AUTHOR OF *RAISE YOUR VIBRATION*

"Forged in love, written in kindness, this book is perfect for any witch who is just getting started and is feeling a little nervous about where to begin. If you follow the steps outlined in this book, you'll be confident in your practice by the time you get to the end. Seasoned practitioners too will love this refresher course, where you're encouraged to open up, let loose, and dive into a nature-based magical practice that places the earth at the center of all that is sacred."

AMANDA YATES GARCIA, AUTHOR OF *INITIATED* AND
HOST OF THE *BETWEEN THE WORLDS* PODCAST

"Phyllis Curott provides an extremely helpful guide to empowering your life through magic, regardless of your experience level. Written with warmth and clarity, *Spells for Living Well* is an uplifting and accessible guide that is sure to assist you in enchanting your life for the better from a highly regarded Witch with decades of experience."

MAT AURYN, BEST-SELLING AUTHOR OF *PSYCHIC WITCH* AND *MASTERING MAGICK*

"From the moment Phyllis Curott bravely stepped out of the broom closet as one of America's first public Witches, she has been showing us how to live both well and magically. *Loving* her latest offering with spells for everything from Self Awareness to Grounding to simply having a Magical Day, along with tips, herbs, oils, and other details honed and passed down to us, all in her upbeat, down to earth, and common-sensical approach to stepping out of the ordinary and into the extraordinary joy of a life well lived."

CARYN MACGRANDLE, CREATOR OF *THE DIVINE FEMININE APP*

"What an absolutely beautiful and uplifting book that makes every day magick not only approachable but also achievable. Phyllis graces us with her years of wisdom and uplifting insight so that we too can manifest our desires into reality. This uncomplicated and effective approach to magick is a must have guide for anyone who is looking to bring more wonder and well-being into their life."

DESIREE ROBY ANTILA, ASTROLOGER AND AUTHOR OF *SUN SIGNS IN LOVE*

"An innovative and enchanting 21st century guide to making magic and working with the powers of Nature, with foundational philosophy for beginners and longtime practitioners alike, from a beloved and experienced Wise Woman Priestess of the Craft."

REV. SELENA FOX, HIGH PRIESTESS OF CIRCLE SANCTUARY

"Phyllis Curott has given us a wise and wonderful book. A positive practical guide that contains ways to reconnect to an earth-based spirituality that is much needed in this 21st century. It is a treasure of simple rituals that are useful for both experienced practitioners and beginners."

BARBARA BIZIOU, AUTHOR OF *THE JOY OF RITUAL*

"Phyllis Curott has created a resource of great power, love, and knowledge to help us journey to well-being, to feel deep peace for ourselves and the world around us, to the magic we all seek. She lays a path for us with this beautiful book, a compendium of spells to help you find both wellness and wonder. An invitation to embrace your own magic and stand in your power to create change, the pages of this book are ingrained with great love and wondrous magic!"

SARAH ROBINSON, AUTHOR OF *YOGA FOR WITCHES*, *YIN MAGIC*, AND *KITCHEN WITCH*

"*Spells for Living Well* is a compendium of magic and wisdom we tend to forget, giving us permission to prioritize ourselves and our wellness, and creating a roadmap for reclaiming our personal power. If you've felt in a rut or unsure of where to go next, I recommend this book!"

TONYA BROWN, EDITOR IN CHIEF OF WITCH WAY PUBLISHING

"There is no shortage of books on magick and Witches these days. Phyllis Curott's *Spells for Living Well* stands out among them. As a Witch of long experience, Curott has penetrated beyond the allure of personal ego to grasp the deeper contexts within which we exercise our will. She deepens our understanding of magickal spells and ability to use them wisely."

DR. GUS DIZEREGA, SCHOLAR, GARDNERIAN ELDER, AND AUTHOR OF *GOD IS DEAD, LONG LIVE THE GODS*

"*Spells for Living Well* is exactly what we need, penned by a wise elder and one of America's first public Wiccan priestesses. The accessible rituals contained in this masterpiece provide the blueprint for 'unleashing the magic' that is essential for all life and Mother Earth. Curott shows us how we can experience the harmony of our reciprocal communication with the natural world and the magic of tapping into the spirit embodied in nature."

PATRICIA FERO, LMSW, PSYCHOTHERAPIST AND AUTHOR OF *WHAT HAPPENS WHEN WOMEN WAKE UP?*

"Have you ever felt a book holding your hand? A Witch, a wise woman, seer, and healer, Curott thoroughly and beautifully restores magic as she weaves us into our deeper connection with all life, the sacred, and nature. Step by intimate step, Phyllis unfolds the process of casting spells for the good of all. If ever you needed a manual to bring to life your dreams of 'bettering' yourself, others, and the world, here it is!"

MARILYN NYBORG, FEMINIST ACTIVIST, FOUNDER OF GATHER THE WOMEN GLOBAL MATRIX, AND AUTHOR OF *A WOMEN'S GUIDE TO SACRED ACTIVISM*

"I loved this book! *Spells for Living Well* is a magickal gem from Wiccan attorney Phyllis Curott, whom *Time* magazine calls one of 'America's leading thinkers.' This wonderful (wonder-filled) compendium is not a grimoire of 'High Magick,' with fancy sigils, elaborate trappings, and expensive ingredients, but a book of practical, simple spells using everyday items for every purpose and especially for Healing, Peace, and Wonder. Each spell concludes with an appropriate injunction to 'Act in accord.' So mote it be!"

OBERON ZELL, FOUNDER AND HEADMASTER OF THE GREY SCHOOL OF WIZARDRY AND AUTHOR OF *GRIMOIRE FOR THE APPRENTICE WIZARD*

"With natural elements such as herbs, stones, and the forces of sacred Earth, Air, Fire, and Water, Phyllis Curott has crafted a practical guide that will be useful to anyone on a Pagan path. Seasonal rituals, Moon magicks, and spells for all the phases and necessities of life are brought together in one simple to use, comprehensive magickal primer. A thorough and useful read!"

ELLEN EVERT HOPMAN, AUTHOR OF *THE REAL WITCHES OF NEW ENGLAND* AND *THE SACRED HERBS OF SPRING*

"*Spells for Living Well* is an enchanting and empowering invitation back into our most natural state of being: Co-creating magic. With spells to soothe, ease, and invigorate, it is a beautiful reminder of what is possible when we remember to weave the magical into our daily lives."

LUCY H. PEARCE, AUTHOR OF *MOON TIME, SHE OF THE SEA,* AND *CREATRIX*

"I love this book! Phyllis Curott invites us to explore the place where enchantment meets practical application. *Spells for Living Well* is more than a guide, it's an invitation to show up in our own unique magic, in sacred reciprocity with our natural world, so necessary now in this evolutionary growth spurt we have the privilege of midwifing. Read this book in the spirit of awe, wonder, and grace. Its lessons and steps are simple, elegant, and medicine for the soul."

SANDE HART, AUTHOR OF *THE LIMINAL ODYSSEY* AND PRESIDENT OF S.A.R.A.H. (SPIRITUAL AND RELIGIOUS ALLIANCE FOR HOPE)

"This latest from Phyllis Curott is a delightful tribute to her lifetime of experience as a witch. From the opening discussion of nature and magic to Curott's invaluable clarification of ethics in spellcasting, the clarity of her prose is refreshing as well as an enjoyable read. A feast for the witch's soul!"

HOLLI EMORE, MDIV, EXECUTIVE DIRECTOR OF CHERRY HILL SEMINARY AND AUTHOR OF *CONSTELLATED MINISTRY*

"Love this book! Phyllis Curott's *Spells for Living Well* takes on one of my favorite questions: What kinds of magic help us live joyful, good, and satisfying lives? There is a new urgency to asking… and answering it *right now*, which is exactly what *Spells for Living Well* does. This book is excellent for beginners as Phyllis begins with spell casting basics to consider before casting your first spell. At the same time, I'd recommend *Spells for Living Well* to more advanced practitioners of the Sacred Arts as the spells in this work are timely and relevant to ALL of us. Enjoy it and begin your magical journey of living a beautiful life today!"

BRIANA SAUSSY, AUTHOR OF *MAKING MAGIC AND STAR CHILD*

"Phyllis Curott has brought mindfulness and common sense to a topic that quickly becomes overwrought for many Witches. Books on spellcasting these days are a dime a dozen. Phyllis brings it back to a more holistic approach —reminding us that magic firstly is a transformative process. It is the unforced and clear voice that sets this treatise above others."
ANDREW THEITIC, ELDER AND AUTHOR OF *THE WITCHES' ALMANAC*

"A deeply connective spell book that combines a how to guide with a deep spiritual connection. It is not your average spell book and is a must have for your magical library."
TWILA YORK, ORGANIZER OF CHICAGO PAGAN PRIDE

"Readers will find in these beautiful pages a key to the most significant of kingdoms: That of our own divinity. Through practical and powerful spells, Phyllis Curott shows us how to enrich, empower, and ultimately transform every aspect of our lives. Many books address the importance of wellness and self-care, but Curott goes much further, teaching us how to use magic to manifest abundance, health, creativity, wholeness, and so much more. *Spells for Living Well* is a book our world needs right now, and one that will be treasured for many years to come."
ANTONIO PAGLIARULO, JOURNALIST AND AUTHOR OF *THE EVIL EYE: THE HISTORY, MYSTERY AND MAGIC OF THE QUIET CURSE*

"*Spells for Living Well* is the perfect tool for the modern, busy but dedicated Witch. Filled with delectable gems of wisdom, Phyllis's voice comes through as the kind, supportive friend—wise and generous. It's a wonderful guide for the new Witch, and a beautiful companion for the more seasoned Witch. Phyllis, once again, has gifted the world with the right book at the right time. I'm just in love."

COURTNEY WEBER, AUTHOR OF *HEKATE: GODDESS OF WITCHES* AND CREATOR OF *THAT WITCH LIFE* PODCAST

"Throughout this delightful book that offers spells to guide one, whether a witch or otherwise, into the magical, natural, and wondrous, Phyllis Curott's underlying premise is that a life without enchantment is one that is not fully alive. Despite our devastated world, this author and interfaith activist, among the very first of America's public Witches, conjures through this literary offering a way for any one of us to live well, harmoniously, positively, and with wonder beyond imagination."

PROFESSOR MICHAEL YORK, AUTHOR OF *PAGAN MYSTICISM*

"We are in critical need of a modern-day prophetess, witch, and mystic. She is Phyllis Curott. In her definitive work, she puts us in simple practice to achieve a magical flow with spirit, harmony, and happiness in everyday life. Curott's powerful transmission casts a spell that at once creates and unites us in a cyclical dance of wonderment, beauty, and abundance with the Mother Goddess."

MAYA TIWARI, SPIRITUAL LEADER AND VEDIC AUTHOR

Spells
for
Living Well

Also by Phyllis Curott

The Witches' Wisdom Tarot
(Artwork by Danielle Barlow)

Wicca Made Easy
Awaken the Divine Magic within You

Book of Shadows
A Modern Woman's Journey into the Wisdom of
Witchcraft and the Magic of the Goddess

WitchCrafting
A Spiritual Guide to Making Magic

The Love Spell
An Erotic Memoir of Spiritual Awakening

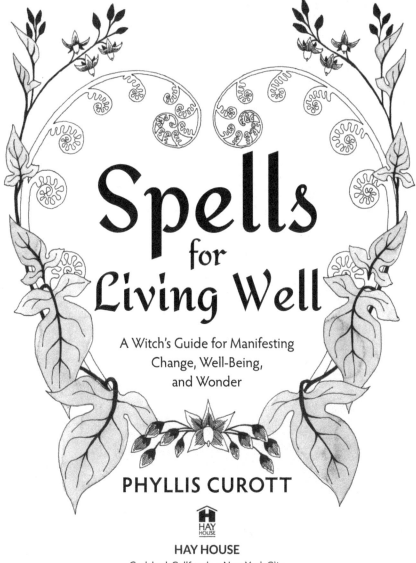

Spells
for
Living Well

A Witch's Guide for Manifesting
Change, Well-Being,
and Wonder

PHYLLIS CUROTT

HAY HOUSE

HAY HOUSE

Carlsbad, California • New York City
London • Sydney • New Delhi

Published in the United Kingdom by:
Hay House UK Ltd, The Sixth Floor, Watson House, 54 Baker Street,
London W1U 7BU; Tel: +44 (0)20 3927 7290; www.hayhouse.co.uk

Published in the United States of America by:
Hay House Inc., PO Box 5100, Carlsbad, CA 92018-5100
Tel: (1) 760 431 7695 or (800) 654 5126; www.hayhouse.com

Published in Australia by:
Hay House Australia Pty Ltd, 18/36 Ralph St, Alexandria NSW 2015
Tel: (61) 2 9669 4299; www.hayhouse.com.au

Published in India by:
Hay House Publishers India, Muskaan Complex, Plot No.3, B-2, Vasant Kunj,
New Delhi 110 070; Tel: (91) 11 4176 1620; www.hayhouse.co.in

Text © Phyllis Curott, 2022

The moral rights of the author have been asserted.

All rights reserved. No part of this book may be reproduced by any mechanical,
photographic or electronic process, or in the form of a phonographic recording;
nor may it be stored in a retrieval system, transmitted or otherwise be copied for
public or private use, other than for 'fair use' as brief quotations embodied in
articles and reviews, without prior written permission of the publisher.

The information given in this book should not be treated as a substitute for
professional medical advice; always consult a medical practitioner. Any use of
information in this book is at the reader's discretion and risk. Neither the author
nor the publisher can be held responsible for any loss, claim or damage arising out
of the use, or misuse, of the suggestions made, the failure to take medical advice
or for any material on third-party websites.

A catalogue record for this book is available from the British Library.

Tradepaper ISBN: 978-1-78817-871-6
E-book ISBN: 978-1-78817-873-0
Audiobook ISBN: 978-1-78817-874-7

Interior illustrations: p.120, 164, 235: Lucy Webster; corner illustrations p.54–62,
88–106, 216–230, 232–240: Shutterstock; corner illustrations p.64–85, 108–149,
168–213, 232–258: Creative Market; p.277: David Benthal; all other illustrations:
Danielle Barlow (www.daniellebarlowart.com)

Give me not words of consolation…
Give me the spell for living well.

THE KNOT OF ISIS
AWAKENING OSIRIS BY NORMANDI ELLIS

Contents

Correspondences and Helpful Information

List of Spells for Living Well

Casting Spells

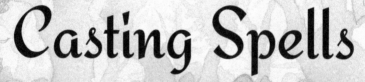

"Most people know intuitively that when you fall in love, the world is full of magic. What they don't know is that when you discover the universe is full of magic, you fall in love with the world."

PHYLLIS CUROTT, *BOOK OF SHADOWS*

A Magical World

"Magic is an essential part of who we are. But sometimes we doubt ourselves. We doubt that magic is real… We need a spell to clear the way, a guide to help us find our way."

PHYLLIS CUROTT, *THE WITCHES' WISDOM TAROT*

The world is full of magic.

We all knew it when we were children. I sensed it every time I climbed into the branches of the apple tree blossoming in my suburban backyard. An old friend knew she'd summoned a thunderous downpour by spinning wildly on a windy hilltop. So many of us discovered magic with a worn velvet rabbit we made real with love. We *knew* there was a wild and benevolent presence watching over us, making magic with us.

Confidence in the magic of a world that's alive, that cares for us and guides us through glorious, bone-breaking, soul-making adventures, fades as we grow older. We pack it away with the rabbit and the fairy tales and pick up textbooks and degrees in order to earn a living, pay a mortgage, and get our own kids to school. Yet a glimmer of the old magic surfaces when we read those fairy tales to them, or to ourselves, or get caught in summer rain, or a dream comes true.

A life without enchantment isn't fully alive. We need the spells that satisfy our longing for love, that nourish our self-care and well-being, that help us find our purpose, our sense of wonder, and spiritual meaning, especially in these troubled times. And as the climate crisis worsens, we're sensing that we can't heal, or find inner peace, or live well, until we've made peace and healed with Mother Earth—until we've learned her wisdom for living well.

We're ready to re-enchant our lives and our devastated world, ready for spells that restore our connections to the Earth, to our spirits, and to sacred ways of living well and with wonder.

Witch, Wicce, Wise One

Perhaps it's no surprise that Witchcraft is the fastest-growing spirituality in America. "Witch" is a word full of magic. Despite centuries of slander, suppression, and misogyny, Witches have reclaimed their wisdom, their magic, and their purpose. They have reclaimed what it means to be a Witch.

"Witch" comes from *wicce* (pronounced *witch-a*), a word that's more than 5,000 years old. A *wicce* (woman; *wicca*, a man) was a wise one, a seer of the Sacred, a shaman of our Euro-Indigenous ancestors.

Witchcraft, the Craft of the Wise, with all its modern reinventions, is rooted in humanity's oldest spirituality, shamanism, and has many similarities to Indigenous wisdom traditions across the world. Wise ones, called a *wicce,* medicine woman, cunning man, *saman,* shaman, *mambo, voelva, udagan, vitke, bruja, strega, fugara, mudang, angakok, bablawo, p'aqo, taltos, sangoma,* and more, have always had similar sacred roles.

Wise ones are healers, midwives of babies, lost souls, and souls who have passed, conductors of sacred ceremonies, celebrations, and rites of passage. They're interpreters of dreams, divinations, and signs, keepers of mysteries, and makers of magic. They're masters of balancing, harmonizing, and uniting inner and outer, the visible and invisible, Spirit and world.

A Witch is a traveler between the worlds who knows the worlds are one. Witches recognize and honor places of power and the spirits of those places. We know the wild divinity of Nature and we know that human nature is better when we recognize that we're part of Nature. We know that plants are healers and animals are teachers and that we have much to learn.

Witches long ago learned that the world was magical. And Witches have always used their wisdom, their skills, and their magic to live well and to create harmony within, with others, with spirit, and with a natural world that's sacred.

I am a Witch. As a Witch who was public 40 years before it was acceptable, as an activist attorney, an internationally bestselling author, and the recipient of honors no one would expect a Witch to receive, I know what magic can accomplish.

Your Power to Cast Spells

Long before the term "manifesting" was popular, spells were an ancient art for exactly that. Witches have always cast spells to manifest, to heal, and to help, and that power resides within *you*, whether you're a Witch or not. You don't have to be a Witch to cast spells, just as you don't have to be Buddhist to meditate or Hindu to practice yoga.

Today, science has confirmed what Witches have always known: Our consciousness has a remarkable capacity to affect the outcome of events. Cast a spell and you tap into your innate capacity to hack your brain, body, and energy to manifest what you want and need, *and* what the world needs from you.

Conjure for love or abundance, health or peace of mind, for change or self-acceptance, and you're taking responsibility for the creation of your life. Driven by your intention, confidence, and belief in your ability to manifest the life you deserve, your spells can indeed work. And though spells sometimes work in unexpected ways, they're always exciting and empowering.

Some people do worry that spells open the door to power that can boomerang, go awry, or do harm. But you don't need to worry.

Spells for Living Well will guide you in spellcasting that is natural, positive, and effective. The spells, charms, and conjurations I'm sharing with you are curated from my teachings and personal *Grimoires*, a Witch's collections of spells and other wisdom, gathered over a divinely magical lifetime, to help you change as you wish or need to, and to live well and with wonder. I hope you'll find it a wise guide to the place inside you where magic dwells, to the Spirit that's always present for you, and to Nature's Great Magic that's blessing you with all you need to live well and to make the world a better place for your having been here.

Cast the spells in this book, adapt them and make them your own, and you'll find yourself manifesting change and well-being. Your sense of confidence, optimism, and joy will expand. Your life will grow and your spirit blossom.

Cast your spells and you'll re-enchant your life and the world.

The Spiritual Power of Spells

Spells have long been used for eminently practical purposes, to bring about changes to make life easier, healthier, happier, richer, and more love-filled. Many of the spells offered here can be successfully approached in this pragmatic way. But spells can offer you so much more, because, if you wish, they can *be* so much more. They can fill your life with wonder because they fill your life with the Sacred.

If you wish to unlock the full, wondrous, magical, manifesting power of spellcasting, work your spells as spiritual practices. Let them guide you to the well of your inner divinity and help you draw that magic forth to manifest gifts and visions that will bless your life and the world. Cast spells as spiritual practices, and they will attune you to the numinous, abundant, life-generating energy of Creation and help you channel that energy into a life of fulfillment, harmony, and magic beyond anything you can intend or imagine.

Cast spells as spiritual practices and you'll discover that all spells are, in one way or another, love spells.

The Magic of Spells

The magic of spellcasting is one of Witchcraft's most powerful ways of manifesting. But what *is* magic? Open most books on spellcasting, magic, or Witchcraft, and you're likely to see some form of this definition: *Magic is the manipulation of unseen, supernatural forces and nature to manifest your intentions and accomplish your goals.*

Like fish that can't see the water they're swimming in, we don't recognize that this idea expresses a very un-magical, patriarchal view of reality. It began long ago when, supposedly, God gave man dominion over an inanimate world to do whatever he wanted with it. It continues in our modern belief that science gives man the power to manipulate and exploit an inanimate world. It's in this definition of magic as offering power over the forces and forms of (inanimate) Creation.

Years of making magic, of slowly becoming a wise one, have given me a very different understanding. Magic is *not* about manipulating supernatural forces, or Nature, or treating the world like an inanimate vending machine. Magic is not about seeking to have power over Creation, or the living beings who live with us, or the forces that make it all work. That approach is *un-natural*, and we're already up to our necks in the consequences of our un-natural behavior.

Cast spells and you discover what the *wicces* and *wiccas* knew:

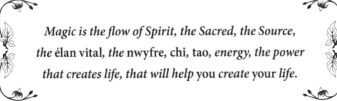

Magic is the flow of Spirit, the Sacred, the Source, the élan vital, *the* nwyfre, chi, tao, *energy, the power that creates life, that will help* you *create* your *life.*

Magic is the source that creates, the force that unites, the flow of divine energy into form and form into energy in a regenerating dance that creates and sustains and re-creates life. Magic flows back and forth, uniting Spirit and Creation, divinity and Nature, and, when we're ready, us.

And magic is utterly natural. We need the magic of living in *this* world where Spirit is present and alive—in the oak tree in our garden, the dog asleep beside us, the partner we love, the ground we walk upon, the life we've been given. Life is longing for us to awaken and to engage with it in deep, loving, supportive relationships that make the world a better place for all Life.

Everything we work with in casting spells—the energies, elements, and embodiments—is alive. Everything is sacred. Magic is sacred.

Cast spells with the divine power that animates all of Creation and you'll find yourself filled with wonder, and your life, your *best* life, filled with magic.

Nature's Great Magic

Everything you need to cast spells for a healthy, abundant, joy-filled life is within you and all around you in the natural world. It's Nature's Great Magic and you're meant to be part of it. Mother Earth shared her magic with me at the end of a long quest—how she creates and sustains life, making Spirit visible—and all living beings live accordingly, except we humans. Confirmed years later by eco-biologists, it changed my life, my purpose, my magic:

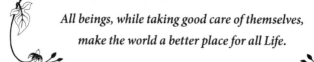

All beings, while taking good care of themselves,
make the world a better place for all Life.

It's true for you too, whether you're a Witch or not, a human or not, casting spells or not. It's deeply spiritual. It's Nature *embodying* Spirit. *That* is the source of magic. That *is* magic, Nature's magic.

As you cast spells, be guided by Nature's magic. Cast spells to live well, to be happy and healthy, prosperous and purposeful, and live a life of meaning and value. Open your heart and the divine energy of life that connects all things will flow into you. Magic will flow into you. It will change how you live in the world and you will change the world. Whether it's a spell, a book, a child, a career, or a passion you pursue, your magic will make your life better and the world a better place for all Life.

Wisdom for Casting Spells

"You are a love spell cast by the Universe."

PHYLLIS CUROTT, *BOOK OF SHADOWS*

An affirmation, a meditation, an incantation, a Full Moon, a feather, a seed, a seashell, a stone, a sunrise—everything has magic and anything can be a spell.

Spells can be written, spoken, chanted, danced, meditated upon, envisioned, performed once or with regular devotion. Spells can be spontaneous and simple or carefully planned and orchestrated. You can recite an ancient Mesopotamian incantation or make up a two-line rhyme. You can listen rather than speak, swim rather than stand, use only your desire or every herb in your kitchen cabinet. You can create an altar filled with everything you need; you can *be* the altar where the Universe casts its spell.

You can start casting the spells in this book right now, but I want to share a little wisdom with you that will enhance your experiences, skills, and results.

A Partnership with Sacred Power

When you cast a spell, you become an energy worker, crafting your life with the help of forces and resources that flow back and forth between the invisible and the visible, between Spirit and Nature, life force and life form. You're *co-creating* with divine powers, with the natural world, and with Spirit.

Spells are a spiritual practice creating a partnership between you and a sacred power that always has your best interests at heart. It sees you in the full measure of your potential, your life, your reason for being here now. It guides you in ways that will fill your life with manifestations of *its* magic: Signs will appear, synchronicities happen, dreams come true; your intuition will blossom, your heart will open, you will sense the presence of the Sacred in your life.

Magic to Discover What You Need

Casting spells is revealing. Spells will help you figure out who you are, what's important to you and why, what your gifts and powers are and how to cultivate them, what your challenges are and how to change them into strengths. Casting spells is empowering. You're manifesting and re-enchanting your life and the world in deeply sacred ways.

But as you cast spells to create a life of well-being, meaning, and purpose, it's important to know that spells don't always offer a predictable result. What they do offer is what you most need. The promise I can make is that whether or not your spell changes your circumstances for the better on the outside, it will *always* work, because you will change for the better on the inside.

Find the lesson within every outcome, and when you do that, you'll realize that everything in life is sacred, both the bitter and the sweet. You'll deepen your understanding of who you are and why you are here. You'll also begin to realize *where* you are.

Cast your spells and they will teach you what you need to know about being fully human and alive in a world full of magic.

Trust

For a spell to manifest, you must be clear about your intention and firm in your conviction that it *will* manifest. But visualizing your goals in detail and being attached to them can be counter-productive. So, when you craft your spells, ask for what's best for you.

And leave room for more than you can anticipate, expect, or even hope for. Experience has shown me that the Sacred intends far more for us than we intend for ourselves. Trust the Universe, trust the Divine, trust the magic.

The Moral Compass for Casting Spells

It's often said that the reason Witches don't cast spells to harm or control others is because of karma or the Threefold Law—a kind of super-karma where what you send out comes back to you threefold. But these aren't real moral principles, they just motivate you to act out of self-interest and fear of punishment.

When you work with energy that is innately sacred, there is no need for fear or punishment. And there is a deep moral compass embedded in Creation, reflecting the oneness of Spirit and world that will guide you. It's Nature's Great Magic, and it applies to all of life, human and other, and to spellcasting, whether you believe the energy you work with is neutral, or supernatural, or gives you power over Nature to manifest your intentions.

Nature has its own innate value, wisdom, and divine strategy for life. Let it guide and empower your spellcasting and you'll recognize Nature making the Sacred visible and Spirit knowable. You'll experience the wise perfection of a divine order where everything in Nature lives well and makes the world better for all Life. Including you.

The Etiquette of Casting Spells

Spells involving other people are generally only performed with their knowledge and consent. In other words, cast a love spell to find the love that is right for you, not to make the guy next door fall for you.

But when people can't ask for help, you can cast a spell offering energy and aid for their greatest good and well-being. Or if they're involved in a relationship with you, cast spells for your own well-being in ways that will also benefit the well-being of others.

What about someone who is doing harm to others? A simple *Quick* Return to Sender Spell (*page 173*) prevents harm and makes life better.

The Four Elements and Spellcasting

It's almost impossible to cast a spell without one or more of the four elements of Nature—Air, Fire, Water, and Earth—just as it's impossible to live without them. The elements aren't symbols or metaphors, they're potent forces of Nature with their own intrinsic value, purpose, and spirit. They're life-sustaining powers that will help you rediscover your own natural, magical powers as part of Nature.

The four elements are organized into a useful framework of energetic relationships called the Table of Correspondences (*page 260*), which you can work with in casting your spells. Each element has a coterie of analogous human qualities, spirit beings and deities, animals and plants, seasons of the year, times of the day, colors, tools, herbs, natural objects, astrological signs, Tarot suits, and more. Don't worry about memorizing them—you'll master them gradually, simply by working with them.

Cast spells with the elements and their energies will flow into the corresponding areas of your life, blessing you with inspiration, energy, love, healing, and more. You'll become whole, more natural, and more connected to Nature's magic.

Here's a brief summary of the correspondences between the elements and our humanity:

Air 🪶 Breath of Life, Mind

Thought, wonder, intelligence, intuition, the power to find meaning and communicate

Feather, owl, incense

Work with Air for: Inspiration, creative thinking, thoughtfulness, communication, peace of mind, calm, focus, learning, writing, lecturing, taking an exam, singing, poetry, cultivating your intuition, consciousness.

Fire 🕯 Energy of Life, Life force

Joy, power, energy, will, courage, passion, transformation, the power to change

Flame, tiger, candle

Work with Fire for: Joy, energy, power, change, transformation, courage, passion, determination, quick manifestation, banishing, purification and cleansing, enlightenment, illumination.

Water 〇 Love of Life, Feelings

Love, emotions, the heart, the power to love and dream

Fin, dolphin, bowl

Work with Water for: Love, dreams, visiting ancestors, intuition and feelings, helping your emotions flow and change, putting out fires of conflict and anger, cleansing and purifying, dissolving emotional blocks, healing emotional wounds, nourishing your inner landscape with self-love, connection, remembering, and storytelling.

Earth 🜃 Embodiment of Life, Body

Embodiment, healing, work, creativity, prosperity, the power to grow and create

Seed, bear, pentacle

Work with Earth for: Manifestation, grounding, nourishing, healing and taking care of your body and soul, the abundant blessings and wisdom of the land, attunement to Nature's wisdom and the cycles of birth, growth, death, and rebirth, cultivating creativity, creating prosperity, giving birth to the life you want.

Timing

The timing of your spells can have an impact on their likelihood of success. Cast them in sync with Nature's rhythms, the great cycles of the Sun, Moon, and Earth, and they will be more likely to come to fruition, as well as bring your entire being—mind, body, and spirit—into alignment with Creation. The benefits are magical.

Seasonal spells work with the life-generating cycles of the Earth and Sun. It's like riding a huge wave—you'll go further, faster, and more easily, *and* feel yourself coming into deep peace and harmony with Nature. Well-timed spellcasting offers you enlightenment and tranquility.

So too when you work with the rhythms of the Moon— your intuition, instincts, and magic will grow, and so will your appreciation for your body's wisdom and magic. Banish during a Waning Moon and manifest during a Full Moon, and you swim with the tides—powerful energies carry you swiftly in the right direction.

The hours of the day, the days of the week, and the seasons of the year all have special energetic significance. They offer an organic, circular pattern of attraction and initiation; growth and accomplishment; release, repose, and reflection:

★ The cycle begins with *Dawn, Sunday, Monday,* the *New Moon,* and *Spring,* with the energies of *creativity* and *beginnings.* These are times for *new projects, plans, divination,* and *wonder.*

★ These energies are followed by *action* and *attraction*, with *Midday*, *Tuesday* and *Wednesday*, the *Waxing Moon*, and *Summer* being times for the work and labor that help you reach your goals.

★ *Dusk*, *Thursday* and *Friday*, the *Full Moon*, and *Autumn* relate to the energies of *abundance* and *fertility*. The harvest time has come, and you can see and experience what you've worked so hard for.

★ Following the harvest is a time of *release* and *reflection*. *Midnight*, *Saturday* and *Sunday*, the *Waning Moon*, and *Winter* are times to banish the negative, release the unneeded, reflect on what you have learned and gained, and make an offering of thanks. The cycle then begins anew, with reflection leading to new beginnings.

Astrological influences can also play a role in timing your spells, as can the relationship between a lunar phase and the seasons, but for now, the essentials provided here will help your spells manifest, empowered by Creation. (*For more, see Timing, page 266.*)

Where

Spellcasting is best done in a quiet, private place. When you can, cast your spells outdoors, immersed in Nature, where you don't have to imagine the elements, the Moon, or Sun, but can experience them and be reminded that everything you need to live well is around and within you. But if you need to put a circle of protection around yourself while on the subway, that's the place to do it (*see* Quick *Sphere of Protection Spell, page 168*)!

Skills for Casting Spells

*"When you cast spells, you become an artist
working with the palette of the seen and unseen,
of Spirit and Nature, energy and life. Casting
spells, you co-create with divinity."*

Phyllis Curott, *Wicca Made Easy*

Spells can be as simple or elaborate as you wish to make them, but let's start with the essential steps and some simple techniques for casting them:

★ Decide on the purpose of your spell, aka set your intention.

★ Decide how to cast your spell.

★ Gather together your materials and tools.

★ Pick the right time.

★ Purify yourself and your space.

★ Cast a circle (often optional).

★ Breathe, ground, and center yourself.

★ Connect to the Sacred (Invoke deity/Spirit).

★ Cast your spell.

★ Set your spell.

★ Give thanks, make your offering.

★ Close your circle (if you cast a circle).

★ Act in accord.

The following accessible skills and practices will make your spellcasting easier, more empowered and rewarding:

Set Your Intention

The very first step in casting a spell is to set your intention—in other words, decide on the purpose of your spell. What's your goal? What would help you live well? State it simply. See it clearly. See its manifestation rather than how it's accomplished.

Decide How to Cast Your Spell

Casting the spells here will teach you how to create your own, and for more help consult the Table of Correspondences and other lists (*pages 260–270*) and see the Sympathetic Magic section on the next page.

Seek Advice First

It's often helpful to use your favorite method of divination to ask for guidance before casting a spell. Simply ask: "What do I need to know to cast my spell?" You're speaking to the Sacred, so the answer will always have your best interests at heart.

If you don't have a method of divination, ask the Library Angel. Simply go to your bookshelf, close your eyes, raise your hand and let it move freely until you feel a pull. Then let your hand fall on a book and take it from the shelf. Open it at random. It will have a message for you.

Rhyme, Rhythm, and Repetition

Spells often use incantations, meaning "singing a charm to manifest the spellcaster's wishes or intention." You don't actually have to sing your spell, but words *are* magic, and they have even greater power when they rhyme, have rhythm, and are repeated (chanted). Here again, ancient wisdom has been confirmed by modern science, which shows that these "three Rs" can have powerful and positive effects on your mind, emotions, inclinations, and your spells' results.

Sympathetic Magic

Spells often work with sympathetic magic—symbolic expressions of what you want to manifest. Essentially, you enact on the outside the changes you want to make on the inside, or in your life. For example, spells for prosperity might involve planting a seed and tending it as it grows, or making a weekly deposit, no matter how small, into your savings account.

Symbols, representations, words, objects, elements, and actions can all be used to express your intention and shape your spell's manifestation. The Correspondences and Helpful Information section (*page 259*) will help you figure out what elements, power objects (*page 41*), herbs, tools, colors, even deities and spirits to work with in your sympathetic magic and in shaping your spells.

Gather Together Your Materials and Tools

See the following chapter for the tools and other objects you may need.

Pick the Right Time

See pages 20 and 266 for help in picking the best time to cast your spell.

Purify Yourself and Your Space

Before casting a spell, it's helpful to purify yourself and your space, unless you're outside, where Nature will purify you. You may wish to purify new tools, power objects, magical jewelry, and other spellcasting aids too.

Most purification is accomplished with the help of the elements, so it's important to be mindful of and grateful for their aid.

Simple ways to purify yourself and your space:

★ Drink water, bringing its purity into yourself (*see Purification Spell, page 57*).

★ Take a bath or shower, or simply wash your hands and face.

★ Burn or scatter a cleansing herb like garden sage, wormwood, cedar, pine, or white sage you've grown or sourced from a local, ethical grower (Air and Fire).

★ Sprinkle salt water (Water and Earth). Although don't use salt or salt water to purify crystals or silver; use a simple solution of water and a cleansing herb.

★ With all four elements: Air and Fire, Water and Earth, as above.

★ Scatter cleansing herbs like those above or black sage, lavender, calendula, and red clover.

★ Ring a bell or Tibetan *tingsha* (pair of small cymbals).

★ Sweep with a broom.

★ Always thank the element(s) for helping you.

Charging

Charging is a technique for filling yourself, an object of power (*see page 41*), or even an element with energy. It can also be done as a spell. Charging with your intention is often called "imbuing."

It's always wise to receive the agreement of any natural object of power first:

★ Greet it with respect, sit quietly with it, touch and hold it, and open yourself to its energies.

★ When you feel it is in agreement, hold it to your heart and send it your intention with all the love and life force that beats there.

★ Thank it for helping you.

A common charging technique is to place the element of Water, a tool, crystal, or other object beneath the Full Moon or the Sun or upon Mother Earth. You can also charge with the powers of the elements by passing the object through or placing it within an element or touching each element to the object or yourself.

Consecrating

Consecrating is a way of blessing yourself, a tool or other object, or your spell.

The simplest method is to lift the object, or your hands, to the Sun or Moon, lower them to Mother Earth and then bring it/them to your heart.

You can also use the purification methods with all four elements (*page 27*) to consecrate.

Anointing

Anointing is the process of blessing or consecrating something—yourself, another person, a tool, a candle, an object—with a drop of an appropriate essential oil or oil blend.

To anoint yourself, dab the oil onto your fingertip and touch each of your chakras. Or keep it simple with just a touch at your third eye, throat, heart, groin, and ankles/feet.

Casting a Circle

Casting a circle is not always necessary, but it can be very useful before casting a spell. Like a pot holding water, a circle holds the energy you work with.

Casting a circle also charges and blesses your spellcasting with the energy of the Goddess. As you work, you'll feel Her nourishment, protection, and love blessing you.

You can also cast a circle as a spell to create a boundary and as a form of protection whenever and wherever you need it (*see Boundary Spell, page 170; Protection Spell, page 168*).

Essentially, casting a circle creates a safe, sacred, and liminal space where you are one with Spirit and Creation as you cast your spells. You can cast a circle anywhere—your home, garden, or place of power, in Nature, or at a sacred site.

Casting a Circle

This can be done very simply:

1. Face East, the direction of sunrise, raise your (dominant) hand (you can hold a feather, flower, rattle, or wand if you wish) and slowly turn around, following the path of the Sun (clockwise, left to right, Northern Hemisphere; counterclockwise, right to left, Southern Hemisphere) until you've returned to the East. You can stand in front of your altar as you turn or walk the perimeter of your circle, beginning and ending in the East.

2. As you turn or walk, visualize a stream of light flowing from the tips of your fingers, or whatever you're holding. Take your time.

3. You may wish to stop in each of the four directions and acknowledge the element of that direction: In the Northern Hemisphere, turning in the direction of the Sun (clockwise), Air in the East, Fire in the South, Water in the West, Earth in the North. In the East simply say, "Welcome, Air," in the South, "Welcome, Fire," etc; in the Southern Hemisphere, also turning in the direction of the Sun (counterclockwise), Air in the East, "Welcome, Air," Fire in the North, "Welcome, Fire," etc., ending back in the East.

4. When you return to the East, see the light sealing shut a full circle around you. See the circle spreading into a sphere surrounding you and the area you're working in.

5.   If you wish, you may say:

> *I cast this circle as a safe and sacred space, a place*
> *between the worlds where the worlds meet, where*
> *Spirit and Earth are One with me. So mote it be!*

Breathe, Ground, and Center Yourself

Like everything in life, spells need energy to work. If you're only drawing on your own, you'll soon find yourself depleted, so Witches usually breathe, ground, and center themselves before casting spells, so we can work with the abundant energies of Mother Earth.

Breathing

Breathing helps clear your mind and calms your body, lowers your stress levels, and enables you to be present in the moment. It opens your heart and connects you to the element of Air and the Plant People with whom you're breathing. It helps you to have clarity as you set your intention and goals.

Grounding and Centering

These important energy practices connect you to Mother Earth (grounding) and the elements (centering), keeping you energized, balanced, and in alignment. They're often used before casting spells, but can be performed as spells in their own right. (You'll be guided through these practices in the Grounding Spell (*page 67*) and the Centering Spells (*pages 61 and 68*). Work outdoors to feel the energies more easily when you begin.

Connect to the Sacred

When casting spells, Witches often draw upon powers greater than ourselves. You may also invite, call upon, or invoke Goddess, God, Spirit, Mother Earth, Source, whatever and whoever is meaningful to you.

To work with the elements, with plants, animals, crystals, and objects of power (*page 41*) you also need to connect with them. Acknowledge their sacredness and *feel* your connection with them. And always express your gratitude.

Cast Your Spell

Don't worry, don't be nervous; there are no mistakes, just chances to laugh and to learn. Open your heart, trust, and let the magic flow into you and through you back into the world.

Feel Your Spell

The stronger your emotional investment in your spell, the more likely it will manifest. Deep feelings energize a spell with a power the mind can't provide alone. But unconscious impulses, anger, or shadow issues can affect the outcome. This may be exactly what you need to know about yourself to make the changes you need. But connect to the positive feelings that make your heart open with gratitude and joy, and your spells will have positive results.

Receiving Energy

Spells often bring energies into you and hold them within you, especially spells for healing, communion, and creating other positive changes. These "receptive energy" techniques, which I call Grail Work because you are a vessel receiving and holding divine energies, include breathing, grounding, meditating, divination, casting a circle, and Drawing Down the Moon (*page 247*). Just being in a circle will fill you with divine energy, and when you're done, rested, recharged, and ready, you should return any remaining energies to Mother Earth (*see Directing Energy, page 34*), with gratitude.

Raising Energy

Spells often direct energies outward, into Creation and into the realms of infinite potential, to manifest. These energy-raising techniques, which I call Wand Work because you are directing energies to accomplish your spell's intention and manifest your goal, include singing, chanting, dancing, running, drumming, or rattling.

When raising energy, you may wish to move around your circle in the natural direction of energy:

★ To create, increase, and manifest, move in the direction of the Sun's "movement" across the sky: Clockwise (*deosil*), left to right, in the Northern Hemisphere, and counterclockwise (*widdershins*), right to left, in the Southern.

★ To decrease, banish, purify, and to perform some kinds of healing work, move counterclockwise in the Northern Hemisphere and clockwise in the Southern.

Directing Energy

When you feel your energy peaking, direct it with your hands into your spell, whatever you're charging, or, if it's a healing spell, toward the part of your body that needs energy. See and *feel* your intention manifesting. I'm always mindful that a living and sacred Universe is receiving my energies, so I direct energy with respect and gratitude, trusting my spell will manifest in the best way possible.

Return any excess energies you feel to Mother Earth. Simply place your hands on the ground and let the energies move from you to her.

To cast successful spells, bring the *right* energies to your effort—respect, reverence, and gratitude—because the energies you're working with are sacred.

Set Your Spell

Setting your spell is like tying a knot at the end of the thread when you're done sewing—it locks your energy and intention into place. One way to set your spell is to say, with energy, "So mote it be!"

Give Thanks/Make Offerings

Gratitude is essential to successful spellcasting, and making an offering is a wonderful way to express your thanks for the energies you have been working with and give something back. When you give back as you have been given to, balance is maintained throughout Creation and there will always be enough for all.

Close Your Circle

Always close or "banish" your circle when you're done:

Closing a Circle

1. Start in the East and turn or walk counterclockwise (Northern Hemisphere, clockwise in the Southern Hemisphere), returning to the East. You may thank the elements at each of the four directions as you go.

2. Envision the sphere of light withdrawing into the circle of light and the circle descending into Mother Earth as an offering of energy.

3. Declare: "Circle is open!" (You may also say: "Circle is closed!" as open and closed are used interchangeably.)

4. You may wish to leave your spell on your altar or someplace safe, but do clean up afterward.

Act in Accord

You can't expect magic, or a spell, to do for you what you're not prepared to do for yourself. Take the actions in your daily life that will help your spell manifest.

The Art and Craft of Casting Spells

"Every natural object is a conductor, a channel, a medium of divinity … they are a bridge between worlds through which divine energies flow."

PHYLLIS CUROTT, *WICCA MADE EASY*

Spells are creative. They're works of art, engaging all of your senses, including your sense of the Sacred, with incense and oils, candlelight and moonlight, ocean water and garden soil, seashells and seeds, flowers and fruits, objects of power and tools, altars and offerings.

As you craft and cast spells with the elements and all the gifts of Mother Earth, rather than using Nature, *work with* Nature. The difference is profound—to use is to dominate and exploit; it's selfish. To *work with* is to enter into a relationship rooted in respect, appreciation, and reverence.

Cast your spells for health and happiness, to live well and contribute to the well-being of Life, and you'll be manifesting your best life in harmony with what's best for Creation. And that's real magic.

Crafting Spells

Many of the spells I've shared incorporate very old and popular magical methods and items that are simple, effective, and easily adapted to almost any purpose or goal. These include:

Spell Pouches or Bundles

These are bags or pouches into which you place the items for your spell, such as herbs, coins, crystals, or stones, a written spell or a sigil (a magical symbol, a pictorial signature of a deity or spirit, or a symbol of your intention or goal). They are often made of small muslin bags, cotton handkerchiefs, or small squares of appropriately colored cotton cloth, knotted or tied with ribbon or cord.

Candle Magic

Candles work with the element of Fire, can have words, symbols, or sigils inscribed or written on them, and can be anointed with oils. Some spells suggest letting them burn down, in which case they need to be placed in a safe spot like a sink.

Potions

Working with herbs (Earth) and Water to make a potion is a common spellcasting practice often used for purification, love, healing, cultivating intuition, and inducing dreams. Potions are commonly steeped as a tea, added to wine or juice, used to infuse a bath with magic, or carried with you in a bottle or, if just herbs, in a bundle.

Incense

Working with herbs (Earth), Fire, and Air, incenses are easy to create and to carry your spell into Creation and the realms of Spirit, and to transform your environment, both inner and outer.

Tools and Other Useful Things

All you really need to cast a spell is yourself, but there are a number of items that will make your spellcasting easier and more creative, and you'll need them for sympathetic magic.

These are some of the common tools and other useful things for casting spells:

★ Pen and paper; a journal

★ A small table for an altar

★ Bowls (silver is wonderful for Moon magic)

★ A broom

★ Candles (use white if you don't have the color for a specific purpose)

★ Candlesticks

★ Herbs (listed in the spells, organic and local if possible)

★ Mortar and pestle

★ A censer, small cauldron, heavy dish or shell for incense

★ Incense charcoal (never barbecue)

★ Essential oils (listed in the spells)

★ Small bottles for herbs and oils, or plastic bags for herbs

★ Salt

★ Cotton handkerchiefs or small muslin bags

★ Ribbons (colors listed in the spells)

★ A small kitchen knife

★ Scissors

★ Matches

★ Birdseed, honey, and other gifts for offerings

Altars

An altar is where you'll cast many of your spells. It's not always required, but it can be very useful and is often beautiful, and always magical. It is an expression of your intention and your creativity. It can be utterly simple or as elaborate as you like, permanent or created for a single spell. It's often placed at the center of your space or circle, or in the direction of an element you're working with.

A permanent altar can be set up anywhere it will be safe and undisturbed, and used for other spiritual practices, reflection, and meditation. It should be given daily devotion and care, even if only for a short time.

You can use your altar to charge your spell, jewelry, a project you're working on, or an object of power (*see below*). You can also create an altar to honor a deity, an animal, a spirit guide, or your ancestors, or as a powerful spell for self-affirmation (*see Celebrate Your Success Spell, page 165*). Your altar should speak *from* your heart and *to* your heart.

Cast spells and you'll realize that there are altars everywhere—a tree that has fallen in the woods, a boulder that was pushed to the seashore thousands of years ago, your grandmother's kitchen table. An altar is wherever you encounter the Sacred.

Power Objects

Spells are often worked with plants (herbs and resins), minerals (crystals and stones), feathers, shells, fruits, seeds, stones, and other natural objects. Natural objects *embody* energy and so they are literally objects of power. A branch may become a wand, a shell may serve as a cup, a stone become a talisman of stability, a crystal hold memories of magic. These objects lend you their power as you cast spells and will help transform your relationship with Nature, with Spirit, and with yourself.

Objects of power are best found in Nature, but can be gifts or purchases. However an object comes to you, it's important to ask it if it is willing to work with you as an "object of power," and if appropriate, to be charged with your intention. Approach the object slowly and greet it with respect. It's helpful to sit quietly in its presence, touch and hold it, and open yourself to its energies. Listen for its voice.

Some beings are very present and willing to work with you and you'll connect with their energies easily. Some will take longer to connect with, like stones, whose sense of time is slower than ours. But every natural object is a conduit of divinity: Spirit moves into the world through it and it helps connect us with Spirit. It *embodies* Spirit. Approach natural objects with reverence, respect, and appreciation, and they will empower your spellcasting.

Talismans, Amulets, Symbols, and Sigils

Talismans, amulets, symbols, and sigils are venerable power objects created for a wide range of magical purposes and spellcasting. They can be utterly simple and natural—a piece of parchment on which you've written a spell, a symbol carved on a candle, a sigil drawn to make the magic, a small bottle filled with earth from your home worn about your neck, an acorn carried in your pocket, or a piece of jewelry, crystal, or a small object for your spellcasting. Whatever form it takes, a talisman, amulet, symbol, or sigil is always charged with your purpose.

Plants and Herbs

Plants are fundamental to life and to many spells. They are also living beings with spirits. They are teachers, healers, and allies. Usually called herbs (resins are a concentrated form), you'll work with them to create incenses, bathing elixirs, magical pouches, potions, and poultices for all sorts of goals like love, healing, prosperity, protection, peace of mind, altering consciousness, and banishing.

Plants, herbs, and resins are also sources of essential oils. Their powers and gifts are blessings—peppermint perks us up, lavender relaxes us, St John's wort improves depression, digitalis helps a broken heart. There is an entire branch of ancient plant wisdom called Green Magic, or Green and Hedge Witchery, much of which has been confirmed by science.

In the Correspondences and Helpful Information section (*pages 260–270*) you'll find a list of essential herbs that you can combine for a wide variety of spellcasting purposes. Some are unusual, but most can be found at local health-food or grocery stores, or farmers' markets. Best of all, grow them yourself. I've included substitutes for herbs or plants that may be difficult to find or that raise ethical concerns, such as (American) white sage, which is being harvested, often illegally, to such a degree that its survival is threatened.

A magically dedicated mortar and pestle is useful for grinding and combining herbs. Remember, it matters what part of the plant you use and how you use it—a leaf might be medicinal, but a root deadly, so it's important to inform yourself about the plants you are working with.

It's also important to be mindful of the impact of spellcasting on Mother Earth. Look for ingredients for your spells from healthy, sustainable sources, find local substitutes for exotic ingredients, and work with the plants found where you live, leaving something when you take something. And be sure to return things to Mother Earth, with thanks, when they are no longer needed. Approach all plants and herbs with respect and you'll be off to the right magical start.

Oils

Essential oils are a treasured and pleasurable part of spellcasting. They are used for consecrating and anointing yourself, your tools, and your spellwork, frequently added to herbal potions and incenses (just a few drops or they won't burn), and rubbed onto candles to enhance your mood and empower your spellcasting.

Aromatherapy has so popularized essential oils that you can find them in your local pharmacy or gift shop. Try to find organic ones, as they have much greater purity and power, but keep sustainability in mind, because the creation of essential oils can raise environmental issues.

Minerals—Crystals, Gems, and Stones

Crystals, gems, and stones are often part of spellcasting, and often treated as if they were inanimate. But, like our bones, they are alive—they grow and change in the same way at the same moment in different locations across the globe. Respect, connect, and work with, rather than use, them and they will empower your spellcasting with real magic.

Crystals will accelerate, amplify, and focus your energies, thoughts, intentions, and efforts, so work with the one(s) appropriate for your purpose. All minerals help connect you to the powers of Earth, to color, light, and energy, and can have a profound balancing effect on your body, mood, mind, and spirit.

As you cast your spells, if they're willing, crystals can be charged with your intention and worn or carried in your pocket, placed in a pouch or bundle, placed on an altar, and worked with as talismans or amulets. In time, a particular crystal, gem, or stone can become one of your most important power objects and spirit allies.

Remember, however, that the mining of crystals can raise environmental concerns, so be deliberate, not profligate, in working with them. And rocks from the ground beneath your feet, rather than exotic crystals from far away, can bless you with incredible power and wisdom. Just leave something in exchange for what you take.

Cleansing Crystals

Don't bathe crystals in salt water, as it can pock them. A mild solution of chamomile or soft soap in warm water will work well.

Depending on their energies, you can also place crystals outside in a safe spot and let them charge or absorb the energy of the Sun, Moon, or Mother Earth.

Color

Color is energy, and important in casting spells. Science has confirmed that differing wavelengths of light—from red, the longest, through orange, yellow, green, blue, and indigo, down to violet, the shortest—have specific properties and effects. Red is the color of power and passionate love; psychologists have confirmed that people feel energized, even confrontational, when surrounded by red. So, a spell for love, passion, or empowerment will be created with a red altar cloth, red candles, and red clothes, stones, flowers, even food. At the other end of the spectrum, blue is the color of peace and healing, and that's its effect on people and how it's used in spellcasting.

The four elements have specific colors associated with them, as do the seven chakras. The Correspondences section provides useful information for working with colors in spellcasting (*page 265*).

Sustainability and Spellcasting

The exploding interest in Witchcraft and spellcasting and the rapid commercialization of plants, herbs, oils, crystals, minerals, and other natural sources of well-being are raising serious concerns about overharvesting, extractive and exploitive practices, and damage to plant, animal, and mineral communities, and Mother Earth.

Always look for herbs from ethical, organic sources, or grow them yourself. Use common herbs rather than rare or threatened plants like white sage, which, as mentioned earlier, has been dangerously and often illegally overharvested. Consider substitutions for oils that create stress on plants and the planet. The increased demand for beeswax candles has led to unethical handling of honeybees and their hives, so consider buying from beekeepers with ethical farming practices or using non-toxic and sustainable candles made with plant-based alternatives such as organic soy, coconut, or vegan wax. And consider limiting your use of crystals, as they are often mined in unethical, Earth-damaging, and exploitive ways.

Nature's magic counsels taking no more than you need and giving back in kind, so that there will always be enough for all. Mother Earth is sacred, so let's strive to cast our spells in thoughtful, respectful, and sacred ways.

The Spells

The Spells

The spells that follow are old and new, quick and easy, slow and deliberate. Some will manifest swiftly, others gradually, some in unexpected ways or not at all. But every spell you cast will manifest the most important magic of all: It will change you. It will give you what you need to know about yourself to live well and with wonder.

These spells for living well address needs and longings many of us have, but the way you experience them will be unique. You'll also find that they're versatile: You can adapt them as you need or want. A banishing spell can be used to help you end bad habits or bad relationships, negative energies or negative patterns, poor health or poverty. An abundance spell can be used for wealth, personal growth, a larger home, success in a career or project, or for expansive spiritual embodiment. A healing spell can help you mend a wounded heart, body, or spirit. And a spell for love can help you love yourself, find the love of your life, expand your experience of what love can be, or rediscover the love of Mother Earth. Make the spells yours and make *your* magic.

May these spells help you change, live well and with wonder, and may you make the world a better place with all that you manifest.

And so the time has come...

Light the candle and ring the bell,
Turn the page and cast the spell...

SPELLS WITH THE
ELEMENTS OF NATURE

*These spells are where all magic begins. They
can be worked with for many purposes, and are
frequently incorporated into other spells. They will
connect you to the healing, life-enriching energies
of Nature and to the natural powers within you.
They are simple, easy to do, and empowering.*

Air Spell for Mindfulness

Air is the element of awareness, the first element you work with when you set your intention and most spellcasting begins with breathing to clear and focus your mind. Breathing is also magical meditation to manifest and to connect to Creation. Cast this spell and you'll discover that the Divine is just a breath away. And that changes everything…

Cast this breathing spell anywhere, anytime. Just a few breaths will make magic.

You'll need

~ A quiet place

~ About 10 minutes

Cast your spell

1. Sit and relax. Close your eyes and take a few deep, natural breaths.

2. Now inhale for a count of three.

3. Hold your breath for a count of two.

4. Exhale for a count of five.

5. Continue breathing slowly, fully, naturally: Inhale, count of three; hold, count of two; exhale, count of five.

6. Feel your body and mind grow still and clear.

7. It's helpful to know that thoughts will enter your mind. Just let them come and go and don't give yourself a hard time. Simply bring your attention back to your breath, and that will bring you back to the present moment.

8. If you need energy, focus on the oxygen moving through your body, energizing you with life. Feel the energy coursing through you, nourishing you, sustaining you, revitalizing you.

9. Feel the energy of Creation coursing through you. You're never alone. Every breath connects you to the Sacred.

10. Continue breathing at a slow, easy, natural pace.

11. When you're ready, open your eyes.

12. Your spell is cast.

Act in accord

Whenever you're tense, confused, or anxious, just take five deep, full breaths and feel your mind clear and your body relax.

Fire Spell for Energy

Fire is the element of energy, transformation, and joy. It's the force of the Sun that makes all life grow; it's the energy of Spirit. It's *your* power to create your life, to change, to live well and with joy. This Fire spell will give you energy to reach your goals, whatever they may be.

You'll need

~ A candle of the appropriate color for your goal (*see page 265*)

~ Matches

~ A small knife

Cast your spell

1. See your goal clearly.

2. Carve a word or symbol for it on the candle.

3. Hold it to your heart. Charge it with your intention.

4. Welcome the power of Fire and its help in achieving your goal.

5. Light the candle.

6. Cup your hands near the flame and feel the tremendous heat that even a tiny flame gives off.

7. Bring the Fire, its energy and light, to your stomach, your power center.

8. Say: "Flame of life within me burning bright!"

9. Focus on the Fire in your belly, the power to bring your goals to fruition.

10. When you're ready, thank the Fire and blow out your candle.

11. Keep your candle to light again when you need the energy to succeed.

Act in accord

Take action to manifest your goal.

Water Spell for Purification

Water is the element of our Oneness. It's the element of love and we cannot live without it. This spell blesses you with Water's natural purity to dissolve any inner blockages, sorrows or suffering, and free your positive feelings, your love, to flow through you and into the world.

The best time to do this is in the morning with the first Water you drink, but cast this spell anytime you need Water's purity and blessings.

You'll need

~   A clear glass of Water

Cast your spell

1. Fill a glass with cold Water.

2. Hold the glass up and look at the Water's clarity, its purity.

3. Thank Water for its blessings. Ask it to help you purify yourself.

4. Drink the Water slowly.

5. Feel its purity moving through you, cleansing you from within. Feel it dissolving and carrying away whatever you need to release.

6. Thank the Water.

Act in accord

Repeat every morning. There's no waste in Nature, so what the Water takes away will feed the fish and nourish the oceans.

Earth Spell for Grounding

This spell is deeply empowering. Connect energetically to Mother Earth and her life-nourishing power, and her love will revitalize, strengthen, and heal you. It will charge you with energy for casting spells and living well and will deepen your relationship with your body and with Mother Earth herself.

You'll need

~ A quiet place; it can be indoors, but outdoors is more empowering

~ A small offering and some Water

~ A tree that's willing to work with you, if possible. You'll know that a tree will work with you when you feel a sense of warmth and welcoming coming from it when you approach it.

Cast your spell

1. Sit comfortably on the floor or the ground, with your back against the tree. Thank the tree.

2. Ask Mother Earth for her help. Close your eyes and feel her presence supporting you from below. Feel her acceptance of you.

3. Sit up straight and feel your back becoming strong and solid, like a tree rooted in Mother Earth.

4. Exhale. Imagine, *feel* yourself sending roots down from the base of your spine into Mother Earth. Gradually feel your roots descending, spreading, connecting you to Mother Earth.

5. Feel her welcoming you, surrounding you, embracing you with love. Feel yourself rooted like a tree in Mother Earth.

6. Now, inhale and feel the energy of Mother Earth flowing into you. Feel her life force flowing into your roots, up your spine, through your body, through your consciousness. Feel her energy, her love, energizing and blessing you.

7. You may feel tingling, or sensations of warmth, light, and energy. Feel her nourishing, healing love flowing into your heart.

8. Direct the energy into whatever part of your body or spirit needs love or healing. Feel yourself being healed, nourished, strengthened, loved.

9. When you're ready, gently and slowly withdraw your roots from Mother Earth, curling them up at the base of your spine.

10. If you feel lightheaded, put your palms and the soles of your feet on the ground and return the excess energies to Mother Earth. (This is also called grounding.) Take your time. Drink some Water.

11. Thank Mother Earth, thank the tree, and leave your offering and pour the Water for the tree.

12. Your grounding spell is done.

Act in accord

Reflect on what it feels like to develop a personal relationship with the Earth as Mother, how it changes the way you think and act.

Centering Spell for Balance

Cast a circle and you cast a spell to center yourself, to create balance within and balance in your life. This centering spell works with each of the four elements and directions to help you see yourself clearly, accept yourself as you are, *and* focus positively for a more centered and balanced life. Cast this centering spell and you'll create equilibrium and well-being in all aspects of your Self as you connect to the wider, sacred world within which you reside.

You'll need

~   Peace and quiet

Cast your spell

1. Stand at what will be the center of the circle, fully present at this moment of your life.

2. Face the East, the direction of Air. Ask yourself:

    Do I think too much or not enough before I act?
    Am I questioning and learning or worrying and doubting?

3. Breathe and quiet your mind. See and accept yourself as you are.

4. Face the direction of Fire—South in the Northern Hemisphere, North in the Southern—and reach up to the Sun. Ask yourself:

*Am I scared or determined in pursuit of
my purpose? What gives me joy?*

5. Feel the rush of energy in the center of your being.

6. Face West, the direction of Water. Ask yourself:

    *Am I in touch with my feelings or am I suppressing them? Do
    I love myself enough or am I giving too much of myself away?*

7. Say, "I love you," and hug yourself.

8. Face the direction of Earth—North in the Northern Hemisphere,
   South in the Southern—and touch the Earth. Ask yourself:

    *Am I working too hard and not taking care
    of myself? What needs healing?*

9. Thank your body and promise to take better care of yourself.

10. Return to the East and take a deep breath.

11. Place your hands on your heart. Feel how present you are. Feel the
    energy at the center of your being.

12. Feel how centered and balanced you are. Your spell is cast.

Act in accord

Repeat this Centering Spell as you need to, checking in with yourself in
each of the directions, honoring yourself as you become more balanced,
more whole, and at peace.

Quick Spells with the Elements

*Cast these spells when you don't have a lot
of time but need a lot of change—to your
thinking, energy, feelings, or actions.*

Air : *Quick* Chanting Spell for Change

The word "enchantment" means "to chant over to manifest the spellcaster's goal." Witches, and Buddhists, know that what you focus on when you're in a meditative state will manifest. So, decide what you want to change or manifest and cast your spell with this powerful chant.

You'll need

~ To decide what change you want to manifest

~ Pen and paper

Cast your spell

1. Set your intention. Write it down—a single word or simple sentence—and hold it in your active hand.

2. Close your eyes and breathe.

3. See the change happening and chant:

> *She changes everything she touches and*
> *everything she touches changes...*

4. Chant until you feel your energy peak and move into the realm of infinite potential.

5. Thank the Air for carrying your intention into Creation. Thank Creation for accepting your spell. Thank She who changes everything for helping you.

Act in accord

Take the necessary actions to manifest your change.

Fire : *Quick* Spell to Recharge Your Energy

This spell will recharge and renew you with the power of the Sun.

You'll need

~   10 minutes

~   Sunlight

Cast your spell

1. Go outside and get 10 minutes of sunlight. Try to do it first thing in the morning, without sunglasses, getting the sunlight on your retina to trigger positive brain chemicals.

2. Bend, stretch, move!

3. Reach up and touch the Sun. Hold it in your hands and bring it to your stomach.

4. Feel the Sun's energy become *your* energy.

5. Thank the Sun for its blessings.

Act in accord

Feel your energy growing stronger and brighter with every casting of this spell.

Water: *Quick* Blessing Spell for Love

Water connects all things. Whatever you put into it goes everywhere. This spell will help you charge Water with prayers for peace, healing, love, connection, or other positive feelings or outcomes for yourself and the world. This is a spell for blessing Water and being blessed by it.

You'll need

~ A clear glass of Water

Cast your spell

1. Fill a glass with cold Water.

2. Thank Water for its blessings and for the life it gives you.

3. Hold the glass to your heart and send your love and blessing, whatever you wish to bestow and receive, into the Water.

4. Drink it slowly.

5. Feel Water's love and blessings flowing through you.

6. Thank the Water.

Act in accord

Pour the Water on your plants or Mother Earth.

Earth : *Quick* Grounding Spell

Whenever you don't have time to sit, but need grounding, healing, and energy, cast this spell.

Cast your spell

1. Stand with your feet apart, firmly planted beneath you. Ask Mother Earth for her help:

> *Mother from whom all blessings flow,*
> *I come to you to help me grow.*

2. Feel her strength and support, her nourishment and love flowing up through the soles of your feet, through your body, to any place that needs healing or energy, nourishment or love.

3. Let Mother Earth's energy fill your heart.

4. When you're done, thank her.

Quick Daily Centering Spell

I cast this spell every morning in my garden. It takes just a few minutes and will bring your mind, energy, heart, body, and spirit into balance, blessing you with all the powers you need to create the life you are meant for.

This is best cast first thing in the morning.

You'll need

~ An offering of birdseed or water, if outside

Cast your spell

1. Face East and say: "May my mind be clear today."

2. Face South (or North in the Southern Hemisphere) and say: "May my energy be joyful today."

3. Face West and say: "May my heart be open to love today."

4. Face North (or South in the Southern Hemisphere) and say: "May my body be strong and healthy today."

5. Face East, reach up to the Sun and down to the Earth and say:

> *Sun above, Earth below,*
> *I stand between you,*
> *help me to grow.*

6. Feel yourself standing at the center of your life, balanced and connected to Creation.

7. Give thanks, make your offering and start your day.

QUICK AND SIMPLE SPELLS
FOR A MAGICAL DAY

The energies of a single day are the small-scale equivalent of the great cycles of the seasons and the Moon. Cast these simple spells throughout your day to attune to and harness these energies, manifest your goals, and enjoy the pleasure of simple, daily magic.

Morning Spell

Dawn or morning is the time for beginnings, making new plans, setting intentions, starting new projects, divination, and wonder.

Cast your spell

1. In the morning, before your day "officially" begins, greet the Sun and pull a card from your Tarot deck to receive some divine guidance as you set your intention for the day.

Midday Spell

From dawn to twilight, the Sun is strong, the Earth is growing, and the energies of action, abundance, attraction, and manifestation are plentiful. Use this time and these natural energies to take action and work to reach your goals.

Cast your spell

1. At midday, take a few moments to get recharged by the Sun.

2. Acknowledge what you've achieved during your morning and then set your goals for the afternoon. And if it's one of those days where just getting out of bed is all you can manage, be kind and understanding with yourself. One small thing is enough. (*See also Spells to Overcome Inertia with One Small Thing, page 191.*)

Twilight Spell

The twilight hours are time to harvest, reflect, and enjoy achievements.

Cast your spell

1. Go for a walk outside, watch the Sun set, and breathe fresh Air.

2. Realize how much you accomplished today and reflect on any insights you had.

3. When you get home, honor and enjoy what you've worked so hard for—sit down to dinner as a celebration.

Midnight Spell

Midnight is the time for dreaming, for inner reflections, release, and rest.

Cast your spell

1. Brew a cup of chamomile tea with a teaspoon of honey and a few grains of salt and spend a few moments relaxing and enjoying it.

2. Take a few deep calming breaths. It's time for bed…

A MONTH OF
MOON SPELLS

*The Moon, in all her phases, is the Mistress of Magic
with her ever-changing silver light and tidal pull
summoning seas and seeds, the lives of women, the
souls and psyches of all who seek her magic. She speaks
to all, changes all, blesses all. Here are four spells for
the magic of each of her phases. Cast your Moon spells
beneath her light and her magic will change your life.*

New Moon Maiden Spell to Set Intentions (Charging an Intention Amulet)

The New Moon, a sliver of crescent that appears at the beginning of every new lunar cycle, is the Maiden Moon, the time of hope, rebirth and energy, beginnings, planning, setting intentions, and initiating projects. This phase is presided over by Maiden Goddesses like Diana, Artemis, Hina, Luna, Ishtar, and Yemanya.

Cast this spell to charge a crystal, a tool, a piece of jewelry, an object of power, etc., with your intention.

Cast beneath the light of the New Moon, and outside if you can.

You'll need

~ A special piece of jewelry, or other object, to charge with your intention

~ A candle of the color that corresponds with your goal (*see page 265*)

Cast your spell

1. Cast your circle.

2. Call the Maiden Goddess of the New Moon to bless, empower, and charge your intention and you.

3. Envision your goal.

4. Light your candle.

5. Charge your Intention Amulet: Hold your object and raise energy by dancing and chanting the spell:

> *What I see, I know can be,*
> *what I create, I know will be!*

6. Hold your Amulet to your pounding heart and direct your energy into it.

7. Lift it to the Moon and feel the Maiden Goddess's confident energies charging your amulet and you.

8. Put your Intention Amulet jewelry on or place your Amulet object where you can see and touch it during the coming month.

9. Blow out the candle and set your spell, declaring: "So mote it be!"

10. Thank the Goddess of the New Moon.

11. Close your circle.

Act in accord

Wear your jewelry or keep your object in view as you plan and act to bring your intentions into being.

Keep your Intention Candle for a Full Moon Manifestation spell (*see page 78*).

Full Moon Mother Spell to Manifest

The Full Moon brings things to fruition, to the fullness of being. It's time for manifesting abundance, love, fulfillment, creativity, whatever your intention might be. At the Full Moon, the Goddess will bless you with the magic of Her presence and Her power. She is Selene, Cerridwen as the White Sow, Freya, and the Inuit god Alignak. Cast your spell by the light of the Full Moon to manifest all that you need to live well and with wonder.

Cast beneath the light of the Full Moon and outside if you can.

You'll need

~   Your Intention Candle or one of an appropriate color

~   Your Intention Amulet

~   A symbol or object of your goal

~   A bowl of Water

~   Something to eat and drink (for grounding)

Cast your spell

1.   Cast your circle.

2.   Breathe, ground, and center yourself.

3. Light your Intention Candle. Place it safely on the ground, (put a glass or hurricane candle-holder around it).

4. Place the bowl of Water on the ground to be charged with the power of the Full Moon as you work.

5. Hold or wear your Intention Amulet and state what you want to manifest. (Love, prosperity, happiness…)

6. Call the Goddess of the Full Moon to bless you:

> *Goddess of the bright Full Moon,*
> *I come to you to seek a boon,*
> *with work and magic, transform my*
> *intention into manifestation!*

7. Hold your Intention Manifestation Object up, or place one hand on your Jewelry Intention Amulet, and raise the other hand to the Moon to charge it and yourself with the power of the Full Moon.

8. Look up at the Moon, repeating the incantation until you feel her powers of manifestation within you. Dance as you chant.

9. When you feel the energy wane, cross your arms over your heart.

10. Ground any excess energy into Mother Earth. Eat and drink to ground yourself.

11. When you're ready to close your circle, hold the Water up to the Moon. Carefully pour some onto Mother Earth. Later, pour your Moon-Charged Water into a clear bottle for future spells.

12. Thank the Goddess of the Full Moon for blessing you as you manifest your spell and your life.

13. Blow out the candle.

14. Your spell is cast.

15. Close your circle.

Act in accord

Take action to manifest your spell.

Waning Moon Crone's Spell to Release and Transform

The Waning Moon is the sickle crescent that harvests. It's time to release, to banish, to end that which no longer serves your life. The power of the Waning Sickle Moon is wielded by the Crone Goddesses, most famously by Hecate. She is a chthonic (Earth) deity who stands at the crossroads of life, so cast this spell and make the changes you need to let go of the past and to move ahead with wisdom.

Cast beneath the light of the Waning Moon, and outside if you can.

You'll need

~ A pot of soil, or a hand trowel, if you are outside

~ A pen and a small piece of paper

~ A towel to wipe your hands

Preparation

~ Purify yourself and your space with salt Water and burning sage.

Cast your spell

1. Cast your circle.

2. Place the pot of soil or, if outside, the trowel before you.

3. Call to Hecate, Goddess of the Waning Moon, Goddess of the Deep Earth, and state your request:

> *Hecate, Wise Goddess of the Crossroads,*
> *help me release [X].*
> *Open the way for my future.*

4. Write down what you want to banish, end or release.

5. Tear the paper into small pieces.

6. Bury the pieces in the pot of soil or in the ancient Earth, and as you bury them, chant:

Take it away, take it away,
Hecate, Hecate, take it away.
Into the past what's banished goes,
the future now will freely flow.
It's mine to make. My power, I take.

7. Thank the Earth for accepting and transforming what you've buried and released.

8. Feel space opening within you. Feel the way opening before you.

9. Thank Hecate. Thank the Earth. Thank yourself for banishing what you need to!

10. Your spell is cast!

11. Close your circle.

Act in accord

Leave the past behind you and act in accord with your vision of your future.

Dark Moon Spell to Divine the Future

The Dark Moon is invisible. It is a time of mystery. It's time to pause, to wait, to remain patiently in the in-between place where the past has gone but the future has not yet appeared. The Dark Moon is when you learn lessons, discern meaning, and become wiser. It is a time for divination. The mystery is hiding in plain sight—ask and it will reveal itself to you. Cast this spell and ask what you need to know.

You'll need

~   A purple candle

~   A bottle of your Moon-Charged Water (*see page 79, step 4*)

~   A bowl

~   Your favorite method of divination, or the Library Angel (*page 25*)

~   Pen and paper or your journal

~   A glass of red wine (or juice)

~   You may also wish to create this Psychic Power Powder or Incense: Use 1 teaspoon each of gum mastic or frankincense, cinnamon, sandalwood, clove, and myrrh

~   Censer, incense charcoal

~   Matches

~   Mortar and pestle

Cast your spell

1. Cast your circle.

2. Reflect on what you need to know.

3. Grind the Psychic Power Powder ingredients together, focusing on your question as you do so.

4. Sprinkle the powder in a circle. Rub a little on your third eye (don't get it in your eyes). Rub it on your hands.

5. Pour the Moon-charged Water into the bowl.

6. Light your candle. Place the candle behind the bowl so the light is reflected in the Water. Sprinkle the powder around the bowl and candle. Light a small amount as an incense, if you wish.

7. Invite the Hidden Goddess to guide you:

> *Goddess of the Dark Moon, Goddess of mystery,*
> *be with me, guide me, answer my question.*

8. Close your eyes. Breathe.

9. Ask your question.

10. Open your eyes and stare into the Water. Let your eyes unfocus and drift over the Water. You may move the bowl to move the flame within it. Breathe and open yourself to receive ideas and images and words of guidance for your next steps. When the visions have passed, write them down.

11. If you need more clarity, use your favorite method of divination or consult the Library Angel (*page 25*). Hold your divination tool

to your heart and ask: "What do I need to know about [X or the message you gave me]?"

12. Reflect on what you've been shown. Write about it in your journal.

13. Pour some wine or juice from your glass into the Water bowl as an offering to the Dark Moon.

14. Thank her. Drink your wine or juice. Take your time. Feel the liminal presence that guides you.

15. Blow out the candle.

16. Close your circle.

Act in accord

Pour the Water and wine or juice on Mother Earth as an offering.

Take the advice you've been given.

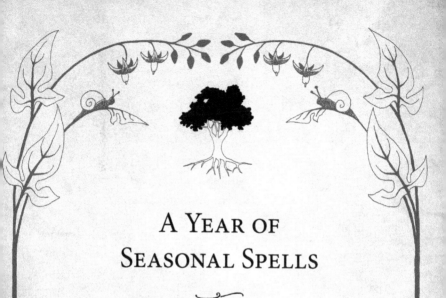

A YEAR OF
SEASONAL SPELLS

❧

*For a year charged with empowering magic, cast one
of these simple spells every six weeks. They will help
bring your life into deep resonance with the energies
of the Sun and Earth, attuning and aligning you to
the rhythm of life-regenerating power. Cast spells in
sync with the great cycles of birth, growth, fruition,
rest and rebirth, and your life will get easier, more
peaceful and productive, and more sacred. Cast
these seasonal spells and create a magical life.*

Samhain Spell to Honor Your Ancestors and Dream the Future

October 31, Northern Hemisphere; May 1, Southern Hemisphere

Honor the past, dream the future! This Samhain spell honors your Ancestors, but can be simply adapted to let go of the past and envision your future. Honoring your Ancestors will help heal familial trauma, freeing you to create the life you want. If the trauma involves sexual or physical assault, begin by working with other guiding and loving Ancestors. Cast this liminal spell as the veil between the worlds of Spirit and Life lifts to prepare for a new cycle of being.

You'll need

~ A white candle

~ A food offering

~ A picture of an Ancestor or beloved person who has passed away

~ A table for an altar

~ Spirit's Guide Incense:

    ▫ 1 part (p) frankincense

    ▫ 1 p sandalwood

- ▣ 3 drops of vanilla oil

~ Mortar and pestle

~ Incense charcoal

~ A censer

~ Matches

~ Seasonal flowers, fruit, and other things of beauty and remembrance

~ A rattle

~ A method of divination

~ Pen and paper, or your journal

Preparation

~ Prepare your ancestral altar in the West or facing West, the direction of the Ancestors. Prepare the incense.

Cast your spell

1. Cast your circle.

2. Light the candle. Put a teaspoon of the incense on the burning charcoal.

3. Face West, place your hand over your heart, then raise your arms outward. See the door of the West opening for your Ancestors to enter. Ask your Ancestors to be with you and welcome them. You may invite an Ancestor to be your aide and guide in the future. You may feel a drop or rise in temperature, see candles flicker, or otherwise sense a loving presence.

4. Sit in front of your altar. Begin rattling slowly to the rhythm of a heartbeat.

5. Ask your Ancestors to speak with you. Open your heart. Tell them what you didn't have a chance to say when they were alive. Using your divination tool, ask them what they want to share with you. Write down their messages to you.

6. Perform the healing magic:

   ▫ Thank your Ancestors for the life they've given you. Without them, you would not exist. Thank them for your life and the blessings you've received.

   ▫ Forgive them their faults. Acknowledge that they did the best they could. Honor the lessons their lives offer you. This may be difficult when you are suffering from ancestral wounds or trauma, but it provides powerful healing.

7. Offer them food and drink. Eat and drink to help you ground yourself.

8. When you feel their presence receding, thank them for visiting with you.

9. You may wish to chant, softly:

   We all come from the Goddess and to Her we shall return,
   like a drop of rain flowing to the ocean.

10. Acknowledge your power to dream a new future.

11. Blow out the candle.

12. Close your circle.

13. Make an offering to Mother Earth with whatever food or drink is left.

Act in accord

For the next six weeks, rest, cast dream spells *(page 134)* and pay attention.

Winter Solstice Spell for the Returning Light

December 21, Northern Hemisphere; June 21, Southern Hemisphere

Inspiration! This spell honors the light that always shines within and celebrates your dream of what comes next. Cast this spell on the longest, coldest, darkest night and discover that darkness is neither empty nor frightening. It's the womb of the Goddess wrapped around you, nurturing you, protecting you, loving you, dreaming you into being. You are the light within Her, and within you is the light of a dream you will bring into being. Bright, precious, perfect—your light is returning!

You'll need

~ 4 yellow candles

~ An altar decorated with seasonal evergreens

~ An offering of food and drink

~ A cup or bowl

~ A candle of the color of the dream you want to bring to life (*see page 265*)

~ Statues of a Mother Goddess and a solar God, if you wish

Cast your spell

1. Cast your circle.

2. Declare your intention with the chant:

   I kindle hope of light returning. Within I feel the Fire burning!

3. As you chant, carve your name and a symbol/sigil of your goal into your candle.

4. Continue chanting and light your candle.

5. Acknowledge your power to kindle Fire.

6. Chant and dance around your altar, holding your candle and charging it with your energy, joy, and love.

7. When you feel your energy peak, put the candle on the altar. Thank the Goddess of the Cosmic Womb and the God of the Returning Sun for being with you.

8. Ground yourself by eating and drinking.

9. Blow out your candle.

10. Your spell is cast!

11. Close your circle.

12. Offer what's left to Mother Earth. Keep your candle for future spellcasting.

Imbolc in the Belly Spell for Hope

February 1, Northern Hemisphere; August 1, Southern Hemisphere

Hope! This season teaches us that no matter how dark or difficult life may be, we can find joy and hope in small things. Life is once again stirring in the belly of Mother Earth, and in you. This spell celebrates the signs of growth within you and your ability to nourish your dream, your bright light, your sense of renewed purpose. You are creating yourself anew!

You'll need

~ 8 small tea lights on plates

~ Your Winter Solstice Candle

~ Matches

~ A pen and your journal

~ Something to eat and drink

~ An altar with seasonal decorations

Preparation

~ Put a tea light on a plate in each direction.

~ Put the remaining four lights in between the directions.

~ Set up your altar.

Cast your spell

1. Cast your circle.

2. Light the tea lights.

3. Write a poem, a short piece, or song honoring your dream, your Fire, in your journal. Read it aloud. Place your journal on your altar to charge.

4. Light your Solstice Candle. See your light growing, your goal, your purpose manifesting.

5. Hold your Solstice Candle and chant:

I am light, in a circle of light.
I am Fire burning, burning bright.

6. When you feel the energy peak, declare you goal and say:

I offer my light to the world!

7. Place the candle on the altar.

8. Ground yourself with food and drink.

9. Blow out your tea lights and your candle.

10. Your spell is cast!

11. Close your circle.

Spring Equinox Seed Spell for New Life

March 21, Northern Hemisphere; September 21, Southern Hemisphere

Rebirth! The Sun is returning, Mother Earth is awakening, and so are you! *Life* is returning—there are little green shoots and buds everywhere. Cast this spell and feel the energy flowing through you. Feel wonder as you experience Mother Earth's magic of rebirth. Your new life is emerging.

Cast outside if possible.

You'll need

~   A cup of seeds

~ Some small pots of potting soil or seed starters

~ A small pitcher of Water

~ Something to eat and drink

~ An altar with seasonal decorations, if you're inside

Preparation

Begin with Spring cleaning—clean away clutter, give away outgrown clothes and things from the past that you're ready to release, including habits that you're ready to break.

Cast your spell

1. Cast your circle.

2. Look around you—how wonder-full Spring is! Hear the birds singing!

3. Sit on Mother Earth and feel the energies of new life flowing into you. Envision the new life you're creating for yourself, the seed growing within you appearing in the world.

4. Hold the seeds and dance clockwise around your circle, charging the seeds with your joy and energy. As you dance, chant:

> *One thing becomes another,*
> *in the Mother, in the Mother...*

5. When your energy peaks, plant and gently water the seeds. Place your hands over them and bless them. Feel them respond.

6. Thank the seeds, thank the soil, thank the Water, the Sun, and Mother Earth.

7. Eat, drink, and celebrate their growth and yours!

8. Offer food and drink to Mother Earth.

9. Close your circle.

Act in accord

Nourish your seeds within, the seeds in their pots and in the world. As they grow, so will you. When the seedlings grow strong enough, plant them in Mother Earth with blessings. Tend them, and yourself, with care.

Beltaine Spell
for Love Embodied

May 1, Northern Hemisphere;
October 31, Southern Hemisphere

Celebrate love! The Sun is warming Mother Earth and she is blossoming. Nature is alive and beautiful, and so are you! It's wonderful just to be alive, to be in your body and in the world, to *enjoy* your body and to enjoy the world. Celebrate the love of the Goddess and the Green Man, and honor your body, its wise and wild desires and its magic. Cast this Beltaine Spell to bring true love into your life and to celebrate your love of life and its love for you.

You'll need

~ Flowers and ribbons of the colors of your spell's intention (*see page 265*)

~ Floral wire

~ Food and drink

~ Birdseed as an offering

Cast your spell

1. Find a peaceful, lovely, natural spot.

2. Cast your circle.

3. Mother Earth is blossoming! Feel the wonder her beauty inspires.

4. Breathe. Ground and center yourself. Feel Mother Earth's sensual, joyful energy running through you.

5. Pay attention to your senses and what you're experiencing. Enjoy how good your body feels, how wonderful and sacred it is. Feel the presence of Spirit in the natural world around you, in you.

6. Weave a crown of flowers and ribbons, and as you weave, envision a heartfelt desire, a dream you want to manifest this year. Feel how you give it life.

7. Chant as you braid:

> *Beltaine magic here I sing,*
> *weaving flowers in a ring,*
> *joy and blessings it will bring!*

8. See your dreams coming to life as your flower crown is created. Sing and dance around the flower ring until you feel your energy peak.

9. Put the crown on, lie back on Mother Earth, and feel her energies coursing through you. Feel the energies of the Green Man coursing through you. Feel the desire for life, for love, coursing through you.

10. Eat and drink and thank Mother Earth for all her blessings, the Green Man for his. Give thanks for your body. Give thanks for love. Make your offering. Your spell is cast!

11. Close your circle.

Summer Solstice Spell for Abundance

June 21, Northern Hemisphere; December 21, Southern Hemisphere

Prosperity! The Sun is at its zenith and Mother Earth's fertility abounds. It's the longest day of the year and energies are flowing into manifestation everywhere! This spell channels the surging, life-generating energies toward your goals as the Summer Solstice Sun empowers you and Mother Earth rewards your hard work with abundance.

You'll need

~ An altar decorated with seasonal fruits and flowers

~ Your Solstice Candle

~ A bowl of Water

~ A small, leafy branch

~ Food and drink

~ Pen and paper

Cast your spell

1. Cast your circle.

2. Breathe. Ground and center yourself. Feel the abundant, life-giving energies flow through you from the Sun above and the Earth below.

3. See your goal clearly. Write it down, fold it, and place it on the altar. See your goal manifesting with abundance.

4. Charge the bowl of Water—lift the bowl to the Sun, touch it to Mother Earth. Using the branch, sprinkle the Water once around your circle, starting in the East and moving Sunwise. Sprinkle yourself with the Water. You may wish to say: "I bless this circle and myself with the Waters of Life."

5. Charge your candle—lift your candle to the Sun, touch it to Mother Earth, hold it to your heart.

6. Light your candle and chant:

> *Sun above and Earth below,*
> *rich with abundance, make my life grow!*

7. When your energy peaks, place your candle in the bowl of Water on the altar. Thank the Sun, thank Mother Earth, thank the Water, raise your glass, and drink. Offer some to Mother Earth. Eat and enjoy the richness, warmth, and beauty of this moment.

8. Make your offering. Blow out your candle and pour the Water on the Earth.

9. Close your circle.

Act in accord

Keep your writing safe and take action for abundant manifestation!

Lughnasadh Spell for Gratitude and Stamina

August 1, Northern hemisphere; February 1, Southern Hemisphere

Gratitude! It's time to celebrate what's growing in the garden of your life because of your efforts. Honoring your progress gives you the energy to keep working to manifest the life you want. Cast this spell drawing upon the traditional Irish practice of offering the first ripened grain to Lugh, God of the Sun: The first loaf of bread from the first grain was broken into four pieces and placed in the four corners of the fields to assure prosperity and to give back to Mother Earth, from whom all blessings flow.

Work outside if you can.

You'll need

~ A loaf of bread, or the ingredients to bake it yourself, if you can

~ Wine or juice

~ An altar with seasonal fruits and flowers, something that represents your work and representations or symbols of your past successes

~ Your Solstice Candle

Preparation

~ Set up your altar. If you wish, bake your bread.

Cast your spell

1. Cast your circle.

2. Place your bread on your altar.

3. Light your candle.

4. Take in the beauty and richness of your altar and all that it expresses about you. Acknowledge your hard work, honor what you've accomplished, and honor your strength, stamina, and resolve to work toward the harvest ahead. Say it out loud (or write your own):

> *I've got this! Yes, I do!*
> *I am making my dreams come true!*

5. Say it again, and again with feeling! A little laughter, please, and a big smile.

6. Bless the bread. Put your hands on it, charging it with your power to create the life you want. Say this old blessing:

> *I bless this bread unto my body.*
> *May it bring me the gifts of health, wealth,*
> *and the eternal blessing, which is love.*

7. Break off four pieces and place them in each of the four directions, starting in the East. If you're inside, go outside and make the offering of bread there.

8. Return, relax, eat, enjoy. If you're outside, pour some wine as a libation (offering) directly onto Mother Earth with thanks.

9. Close your circle.

Autumn Equinox Harvest Spell

September 21, Northern Hemisphere; March 21, Southern Hemisphere

Harvest abundance and wisdom! Honor the generosity of Mother Earth. Honor what you've accomplished and the well-being you've created in bringing your dreams to life. Harvesting also means cutting away the things that no longer serve your life. Learn the lessons from this cycle of growth and you'll find the seeds of your future. Cast your spell and give thanks for all the abundance and blessings you've received and created.

You'll need

~   Your Solstice Candle

~   Matches

~ An ear of corn

~ Pen and paper, or your journal

~ An altar of seasonal abundance and beauty

~ Something to eat and drink

Cast your spell

1. Cast your circle.

2. Breathe. Ground and center yourself. Feel the power to manifest abundance flow through you.

3. Light your candle.

4. Acknowledge yourself and what you've accomplished. What have you created? What is your harvest? If there's more work ahead, acknowledge your strength and capacity to press on.

5. Reflect on the lessons life has offered you over the last year. What no longer serves your growth and happiness? Journal your reflections.

6. Close your eyes and envision how your life will change once you have released the things that no longer serve your well-being.

7. Cut away the old: Take the corn and strip the husk and protective green sheaf from it.

8. Study the corn closely. See how many kernels of corn have grown from a single kernel planted and tended by someone who cared, and blessed by Mother Earth, the Sun and the elements.

9. What have you learned about yourself as you have manifested your life? What is the seed of your next cycle of growth? Write your insights in your journal.

10. Give thanks for your harvest and all of the blessings you've received and created.

11. Eat, drink, and congratulate yourself.

12. Make your offering.

13. Let your candle burn down in a safe place.

14. Close your circle.

ABUNDANCE SPELLS

Mother Earth embodies the Law of Abundance—from one apple seed planted and tended with care, an apple tree will grow, producing thousands of apples with thousands more seeds for thousands more trees with thousands more apples for generations to come. Just remember to give back in kind for what you've been given and there will always be enough for everyone.

Count Your Blessings Spell

How can we ask for more if we're not grateful for what we already have? This is a spell to awaken your awareness and gratitude for all the blessings you already have, for the success you've already achieved, the gifts you've been given. It's a spell of mindfulness and generosity, of harmony and balance. Cast this spell to remind yourself that you are always loved, nourished, and supported by Nature's divine magic, and that magic, even when it is about self-care, is never selfish.

Cast your spell

1. Consider all that you've been given.

2. Each day for a week, write down one thing for which you're grateful.

3. For each gift that you've received or reward you've gained, choose a way to give back.

Act in accord

Small acts have a large impact. Whatever you choose to do, do it with fullness of spirit and heart. Watch your life flourish.

Quick Prosperity Spell

Most of us are blessed with truly abundant lives, but there are times when we need more than we have or we're ready to enjoy more. Cast this spell to experience more of life's natural, magical, expansive generosity.

This spell is best cast at the Full Moon or under the midday Sun during Summer.

You'll need

~ A large green candle

~ A small knife

~ Some bay leaves

~ A plate

~ Matches

Cast your spell

1. Set your intention for greater prosperity clearly.

2. Carve a large green candle with your name and a large dollar (euro or other currency) sign.

3. Set the candle on a plate of bay leaves arranged like rays of the Sun or petals of a flower, radiating outward from the candle.

4. Light the candle and repeat this Prosperity Spell until you feel your inner energies shift and the blessings of abundance, prosperity and the generosity of Mother Nature flowing to you.

> *Mother from whom all blessings flow,*
> *help me make my prosperity grow*
> *with work that I love for which I'm well paid,*
> *helping myself and others with all I've made.*

5. Set your spell by declaring: "So mote it be!"

6. Let your candle burn out, in a safe spot. Keep any melted wax and the bay leaves as an amulet of prosperity on your altar or someplace safe.

Act in accord

Cast the Gratitude Spell (*page 242*) to keep your energies positive until the spell manifests.

When prosperity comes, return the bay leaves to Mother Earth, dispose of the wax, and give something back to those who have less.

Money-Drawing Spell for Financial Well-Being

This is a very old spell from a very old *Grimoire*, beloved by many Witches. Just remember to begin with gratitude for what you already have and to give back as generously as you receive.

Cast this spell three times: First on the first night of the New Moon at the exact hour of midnight, again at the Half-Moon at midnight, and finally at the midnight hour of the first night of the Full Moon.

You'll need

~ A Money-Drawing Powder made with equal parts:

　◻ Powdered frankincense

　◻ Heliotrope

　◻ Tonka (you can substitute deer's tongue, woodruff, or vanilla bean for tonka)

~ A mortar and pestle

~ A green candle

~ Matches

~ 3 silver coins

Cast your spell

1. Begin on the night the New Moon crescent appears in the night sky. It's important to see the Moon, so if you must work indoors, go outside first, reach up and hold it between your hands. Bring it to your heart. Return indoors and continue.

2. Grind the herbs together clockwise, focusing on your intention of drawing money and prosperity to you. Make enough for three spell workings. Keep the rest in a labeled jar out of the sunlight.

3. Rub the Money-Drawing Powder on your hands, your feet, the candle, and the coins. Rub some on your wallet, your checkbook, your desk or workspace.

4. At exactly the hour of midnight, light the green candle and take it in your left hand. Take the three silver coins in your right hand and go forth into the night, if you can. Stand in the rays of the moonlight, or bring it back inside with you.

5. Place your candle on the Earth/ground.

6. Lift your face to gaze upon the Moon and say:

> *Greetings, Lady of the Moon,*
> *Gracious Goddess, I bow before you and ask a boon.*

7. Bow to the Moon.

8. Hold your palms outstretched with the coins toward the Moon and say:

I turn this silver beneath your light
and ask for abundance with this ancient rite.

9. Turn each coin over three times.

10. Bow again to the Moon. Carry your candle back inside and extinguish the flame. Keep your coins in a safe place.

11. Cast the same spell at the midnight hour of the Half-Moon, relighting the candle and working with the same coins.

12. Cast again at the midnight hour of the first night of the Full Moon. Thank the Lady of the Moon.

13. Allow your candle to burn down.

14. Your spell is cast!

Act in accord

Keep your coins on your altar or deposit them in your savings account.

Take actions to manifest wealth and return the blessing when it arrives.

Apple Tree Abundance Spell

Trees are generous teachers; they'll show you Nature's secret magic, and how simple it is to live well because you live in accord with Mother Earth. This is an old spell from the West Country of England for giving and receiving blessings. Cast it to manifest abundance by honoring apple trees with gratitude and offerings.

It is best cast, as it continues to be in England, on Twelfth Night (January 6th).

You'll need

~ A cake (it's best if you bake it yourself)

~ Cider

~ An apple tree that welcomes you

Preparation

~ Find an older apple tree to work with.

~ Bake your cake, if you wish.

Cast your spell

1. Greet the apple tree and its spirit.

2. Make your offering to the apple tree and its spirit:

~ Place your cake on its branches.

~ Pour the cider on its roots.

3. As you make your offering, say the old blessing charm:

> *Here's to thee, old apple tree.*
> *Whence thou mayest bud, and whence thou mayest blow.*
> *And whence thou mayest bear apples enow!*
> *Hats full! Caps full!*
> *And my pockets full too!*
> *Hurrah-ya!*

4. Say this new spell as well:

> *Breathe with me, old apple tree.*
> *I offer my breath, as yours to me.*
> *From one apple, many seeds,*
> *from many seeds, an orchard grows,*
> *beauty, life, and spirit flourish.*
> *Receive my thanks for all you nourish.*

5. Sit beneath the apple tree. Enjoy your time together.

6. When you're ready, thank the apple tree and leave with blessings.

Act in accord

Cultivate your relationship with the apple tree, visiting it and making offerings of cake, cider, and Water charged with love, poured out in a circle below the furthest reach of the tree's branches.

Singing and dancing around the apple tree will also help it to recover from any illnesses and to grow strong and live long.

A similar blessing spell can be cast with other trees. Learn about their magic and the traditional offerings made to them.

Old Italian Amulet Spell for Good Luck

Published in *Etruscan Roman Remains* in 1892 by American folklorist Charles Godfrey Leland, who spent the last years of his life in his beloved Italy, this is a spell for a dreaming amulet that will bring good luck. Cast it and may sweet dreams and *buona fortuna* manifest.

You'll need

~ 2 twigs or small sticks from an oak tree

~ A piece of red wool, approximately 1 foot (⅓ meter) long

Cast your spell

1. Thank the oak tree from which you have taken the twigs or sticks.

2. Lay the twigs across each other to make an "X."

3. Wind the red wool around where they cross, binding them together.

4. Hold your amulet to your heart to charge it with your intention to manifest good luck and good fortune.

5. Place your amulet beside your bed and before going to sleep, repeat:

> *Non metto questo quercia,*
> *ma metto la fortuna,*
> *che non possa abbandonar,*
> *mai la casa mia.*

> *('Tis not oak which here I place,*
> *but good fortune—by its grace,*
> *may it never pass away,*
> *but ever in my dwelling stay.)*

6. *Buona fortuna!* Your spell is cast.

Act in accord

In the morning, hang your amulet in your home to bring good luck.

When good fortune arrives, unbind the sticks and return them to the tree with thanks. And share some of your good fortune with someone less fortunate.

Manifestation Spell for a Boon

A boon is a favor you've asked of the Spirit of Creation. It's something beneficial and rare, and when it happens, it's a gift from a living Universe that cares about you and your well-being.

Because this is a special spell, I'm sharing two special spellcasting boons from the first, very old *Grimoire* I received:

~ A Manifestation Oil that can be added to any spell to enhance its probability of success. Use it to anoint yourself, your candles, and your spellcasting objects; add a drop to your potions and your bath Water.

~ A magical technique for anointing spell candles.

Cast this spell when you're in need of more, whether it's energy, wealth, health, happiness, or something else that contributes to your well-being. Remember, self-care is never selfish—just remember Nature's magic and give back as you have been given to and you'll contribute to the abundance and well-being of the world.

You'll need

~ A candle of the appropriate color for the boon you are requesting (*see page 265*)

~ Matches

~ A small knife

~ The Manifestation Oil, for which you'll need the following, mixed to your liking:

  ▢ Vetiver oil

  ▢ Jasmine oil

  ▢ Myrrh oil

  ▢ A pinch of cinnamon

~ A small bottle and funnel

Cast your spell

1. Ask for your boon:

> *I ask the Universe/Spirit of Creation/Goddess/*
> *God for the boon of [your request].*

2. Inscribe a five-pointed star (pentagram) on the candle.

3. Add your name and a word or symbol of the boon.

4. Anoint the candle with the Manifestation Oil. Anoint from the middle of the candle upward toward the wick and the Sun, then anoint downward from the middle of the candle toward yourself and the Earth, continuing up and down, all the way around the candle as follows:

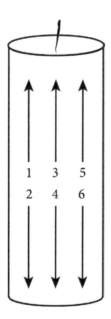

5. As you anoint your candle, see the boon manifesting in your life. See yourself being blessed with greater well-being.

6. Now light the candle, thinking of the spell having worked successfully.

7. Let the candle burn down.

8. Express your gratitude to the sacred energies you've asked for the boon.

Act in accord

Pay attention to the power and presence of the Divine in your life, nourishing, supporting, and blessing you and all of Creation, and give back in kind in gratitude for what you've received.

LOVE SPELLS

Love is the greatest magic. It's all around you,
it's within you, it's ready to arrive when you're
ready to receive it and to give it. Open your
heart to the Universe and magic happens.

Love Yourself Spell

Love yourself and you'll be able to love another person who's able to love you. A light will shine within you. It's the beauty of your heart showing itself to the world and it makes the world a better place. Cast this spell and fill your life with a renewed sense of well-being, peace, and contentment, and with well-deserved self-love.

This spell is best cast on a Friday night with a Full Moon, but any time will do.

You'll need

~ An altar to love

~ A pink candle

~ Matches

~ Pen and paper

~ A glass of good red wine (or juice)

~ A small mirror

~ The ingredients for a Love Incense:

  ▫ Musk root powder

  ▫ Ambroxide or Ambroxan (modern replacement for ambergis)

  ▫ Patchouli oil

  ▫ Rose oil

~ A mortar and pestle

~ Incense charcoal

~ A censer

Preparation

~ Create an altar to love with pictures of yourself that you love, examples of your accomplishments, and representations of what you value about yourself, the things you love to do, and the people, animals, and things you love, including your favorite flowers, fruit, and food.

~ Create your Love Incense, grinding clockwise with the mortar and pestle. Enjoy yourself doing it.

~ Put a teaspoon of the incense on a burning charcoal.

Cast your spell

1. Cast your circle.

2. Breathe. Ground and center yourself. Feel the love of Mother Earth filling you.

3. Set your intention to love yourself, to love your life, and if you wish, to share love with the right person for you.

4. Call upon the aid and blessing of Mother Earth, Demeter, Hera or another love deity.

5. Close your eyes and connect with the child within yourself. Tell that child that you love them. *Feel* your love flowing to yourself as

a child. Feel it flowing back to yourself as the adult responsible for that child, for yourself as an adult. Say:

I love and care for myself. I'm deserving of love,
able to give myself love, able to receive that love.

6. Carve a heart sigil on your candle. Hold it to your heart and charge it.

7. Pour yourself a glass of red wine or juice. Toast yourself and drink.

8. Write a love letter to yourself. Include all the good things about yourself that you value. Include the gold in the dark—the positive gifts that your defenses, shadows, or self-doubts have given you. Take your time. See the best of yourself with love and generosity.

9. Put your thumb in the wine and press your thumbprint into the letter.

10. Read your letter out loud.

11. Give yourself a hug, look at yourself in the mirror and see the light shining in your eyes.

12. Honor and toast yourself out loud with the words: "I love myself!"

13. Thank the deity of love for blessing you and your spell.

14. Close your circle.

Act in accord

Offer the rest of the wine or juice to Mother Earth. Take good care of yourself and reread your love letter to yourself to reinforce your spell.

True Love Spell

Love is the greatest magic there is. There's more love than you'd ever imagine, filling the world and blessing us in more ways than we could ever imagine. Love is a spell that the Universe cast when it created us, when it created *you*. The love you long for has been within you from the beginning. Open your heart, cast your spell, be patient and certain, and love will arrive…

This spell is best cast on a Friday evening when the Moon is Full.

You'll need

~   A love altar filled with abundant and voluptuous beauty

~   A red candle

~   Matches

~   Pen and paper

~   A glass of good red wine (or juice)

~   A small mirror

~   Love Incense (*see previous spell*)

~ A mortar and pestle

~ Incense charcoal

~ A censer

Preparation

~ Create your altar.

~ Burn your Love Incense.

Cast your spell

1. Cast your circle.

2. Invoke the aid and blessing of a deity of romantic love like Aphrodite or Eros. You might say:

Goddess of love, I seek my true love,
who's been within me all along.
Aid my spell and bring her/him/them to my arms!

3. Carve a heart sigil on your candle.

4. Light your true love candle.

5. Write a love letter to the person who is your true love. Describe their good qualities, how they love yours, why they're the right person for you, why they will make you happy, and why you love them and will make them happy. Sign your letter.

6. Read your letter aloud and allow yourself to feel the joy of being with your true love.

7.   Toast your love and declare:

> *My love, you've been within me all along.*
> *I cast this spell to bring you to my arms!*

8.   Put your thumb in the wine and press your thumbprint to your letter to set your spell.

9.   Your love spell is cast.

10. Close your circle.

Act in accord

Offer the wine or juice to Mother Earth.

Keep your love letter spell on your altar or somewhere safe. Reread it when the Moon is Full.

Take good care of yourself as a continuing spell to love, and live well.

Be patient. Love will come.

Venus Love Potion Spell

This is a variation of the famous spell for erotic, passionate love, one of the divine blessings of being alive. Invoke Venus, Aphrodite, the orishas Oshun or Yemeya, Astarte, Bastet, Milda, Branwen, Freyja, Kamadeva, Dionysus, or Eros, from whom the word "erotic" comes. Cast this spell and enjoy the embodied magic of love.

You'll need

~ A Venus Love Potion:

   ◙ 1 teaspoon each of almond, patchouli, jojoba, musk, and rose essential oils

   ◙ A pinch of cinnamon (or red pepper)

   ◙ A pinch of damiana (or nutmeg)

~ A bathtub

~ A red candle

~ Red roses

Cast your spell

1. Mix the oils, herbs, and spices together to create a perfume you respond to.

2. Run a warm bath.

3. Invite a deity of erotic love to bless your desire with fulfillment.

4. Light your candle. Turn off the lights.

5. Take off your clothes, look in the mirror and admire yourself. Your body is beautiful. You are beautiful.

6. Pour the Venus Love Potion into the bath. Add the roses.

7. Enter the bath and let yourself sink gently into the Water's warm and welcoming embrace. Feel the silky texture of the Water against your skin; feel the silkiness of your skin.

8. Run the tub Water to keep it hot enough. Feel the churning power of the Water against your body.

9. Close your eyes and imagine yourself with someone who arouses and satisfies your deepest desires. Give yourself joy and enjoy yourself.

10. When you're ready, open your eyes. Send your love into the Water to be carried to the person who is meant for you.

11. Thank the Water, the herbs, the roses. Thank your body and your imagination.

12. Get out of the tub. Your love spell is cast.

Act in accord

Relax, listen to music. Enjoy something delicious and the blessings of your beloved and beautiful body. Offer the rose petals to the ocean, or to Mother Earth.

Deepen Your Love Potion Spell

People have been seeking love potions since the beginning of time. They're the magic most often asked for, but love *is* the greatest magic. Cast this very old love powder spell to awaken, deepen and magnetize the love you've found within yourself or with another.

This is best cast when the Moon is Full.

You'll need

~   Vervain

~   Periwinkle

~   Food, wine, or juice

Cast your spell

1.   Make a mixture of vervain and periwinkle, using equal parts of a teaspoon of each.

2.   Add 2 pinches of the mixture to food or wine.

3.   If you add the potion to wine, let it steep for 12 hours, then strain it before drinking it or sharing it with your loved one.

Act in accord

Enjoy yourself, enjoy your beloved, enjoy love. Remember, you are a love spell cast by the Universe.

Quick True Love Charm

There is old wisdom that says your true love has been with you since before you were born, living in your heart. Cast this very old spell when you're ready to manifest true love in your life.

You'll need

~ A red flannel bag or fabric square and a red ribbon

~ A lodestone

~ A piece of orris root

~ A mandrake twig (or a pinch of natural tobacco)

~ Vervain

~ Periwinkle

~ Mint

~ A red rosebud

Cast your spell

1. Set your intention to bring your true love into your life and into your arms.

2. Fill the red flannel bag or fabric square with the lodestone, orris root, mandrake twig or tobacco, some pinches of vervain, periwinkle, and mint, and the red rosebud. Thank the plants for aiding you.

3. Close the bag or the square with the red ribbon knotted 9 times. Hold it to your heart and charge it with your love.

4. Your spell is cast.

Act in accord

Carry the bag with you. Be patient. True love can take time, self-awareness, and maturity to materialize and the other person must also be ready. When they appear, open the bag and return the contents to Mother Earth with thanks.

Spell to Make a Dream Come True

Love comes in all shapes, sizes, and species, in all sorts of reasons to be grateful, in all the things you dream of most deeply. Signs may be appearing, synchronicities signaling, unexpected magic manifesting. The atmosphere around you may be charged with a sense of presence and portent. The things you've only dreamed of may be within reach. This is the spell to make your dreams come true.

You'll need

~ A dream

~ Pen and paper

~ The New Moon

Cast your spell

1. When the New Moon appears in the night sky, write a short rhyming spell for a dream you long to manifest in the world.

2. Go out and feel the rush of excitement, of possibility, that the silver crescent evokes in you. It has appeared from darkness, full of the promise of what's to come.

3. Envision your dream coming true. *Feel* what it will be like for it to manifest.

4. Reach your arms up to the Moon and ask Selene, Goddess of the Silver Crescent, to help you bring your dream to life.

5. Chant your spell, beginning slowly and softly. The words may sound strange and you may feel shy, but as you chant, your confidence will grow.

6. Chant louder, faster, stronger. Chant with all the open-heartedness of the child you once were, the child that knew anything was possible and that magic was real.

7. Chant into the magic of the Moonlit night.

8. Chant and feel your dream being charged with the power of the New Moon.

9. Chant your spell until you feel your energy peak, then chant more slowly, more quietly. Chant until your spell disappears into the night, into realms of Spirit and Infinite Potential.

10. Give thanks to Selene, Lady of the New Moon.

11. Crouch down and touch Mother Earth who gives life to Spirit and to dreams. Thank her.

12. Your spell is cast.

13. Go to bed. A spell well begun is half done...

Act in accord

In the morning and every morning that follows, act in accord to bring your dream into being.

SPELLS FOR PURIFICATION, CLARITY, AND CHANGE

Life inevitably sends crises our way. Bad habits take hold and messes accumulate. Relationships go awry and sorrow lingers too long. We can't control the challenges, but we can control how we respond— we can clear away what stands in the way of our well-being. Banishing spells can work with the force of a Spring wind blowing through a house shut up all Winter long. But cleaning out your emotional attic can take time, patience, and persistence. These purification spells will help you banish blocks and negativity and open the flow of positive energies.

Banishing the Blockages Spell

This is the classic banishing spell to free yourself from whatever or whomever you need to—people, problems, emotions, negativity, or blockages that stand between you and your health, happiness, and well-being. Cast this spell to banish negativity and call positivity into the space you've opened to receive it.

You'll need

~ A blue candle

~ A small knife

~ A pen and small piece of paper

~ An ashtray or cauldron

Cast your spell

1. Set up your altar and set your intention to banish your blockages.

2. Cast your circle.

3. Write what you need to banish on the paper—the name of a wounding person or a few words describing the pattern, habit, negativity, or problem.

4. Declare that it's time for you to be free, happy, healed—whatever the positive reality is.

5. Carve: "Free from [X]!" on your candle.

6. Light the candle.

7. Light the paper.

8. Chant:

> *Away, away, away [X] goes.*
> *To me [power, happiness, freedom, healing, etc.] flows!*

9. As the paper burns, drop it safely into the ashtray and continue chanting.

10. Feel whatever you're banishing burn away with the paper.

11. Stretch and reach and move!

12. Feel the lightness inside you, the ease of your body moving on the outside.

13. Thank the Fire and blow out your candle.

14. Your banishing spell is cast!

Act in accord

~ Take whatever is left of the ashes outside.

~ Hold the ashes in the palm of your hand. Feel how weightless they are.

~ Take a deep breath and blow them away.

~ Repeat the spell as necessary.

Sweep It Clean Spell

Places hold energy. Your home contains yours, good and bad. This spell will help you clean, de-clutter and banish whatever needs to go. Sweep away the stale and negative and open your space and your life to the flow of positive energy, optimism, and well-being.

You can use this spell to sweep away bad habits, bad relationships, mental confusion, and just about anything you need to get out of your home and your life.

This is best cast on a beautiful day, preferably in early Spring, but you can do it whenever you need to—midnight on a moonless night in the middle of a raging storm can be very cleansing.

You'll need

~ A broom

Cast your spell

1. Open all the doors and windows in your home.

2. Stand at your front door, pick up your broom, and take a deep breath.

3. Focus on your intention:

Out with (the old) and in with [the new]!

4. Start at the front door and sweep the negativity out! (Either sweep the actual dust and dirt out along with the energies, or just sweep out the energies by holding the broom a little way from the floor, walls, and ceilings.)

5. Move counterclockwise, sweeping along the floors, ceilings, and walls of all your rooms. Sweep, sweep, sweep! Sweep the gunk out the windows! Chant as you sweep:

> *Sweep away, sweep away, sweep away the old.*
> *Sweep away the must and the dust and the mold.*
> *Sweep away the tears and the fears and the sorrow.*
> *I'm clearing the energies for a happy tomorrow!*

6. Sweep the negative energies out of the windows.

7. Sweep until you've come full circle back to the front door. Sweep the last of any lingering negativity out of the door.

8. Close the door!

9. Lay your broom across the threshold to seal and set you spell. You may say:

> *My home is cleansed and so am I!*

10. Go to each window, breathe deeply, and welcome the fresh clean Air, its clarity and inspiration into your home. As you go, say:

> *Clean and bright, flow, positive energy,*
> *into my home and into me!*

11. Close each window.

12. Back at your front door, pick up your broom and put it away.

13. Your spell is cast.

Act in accord

Keep your space—in your head, your heart, and your home—clear and uncluttered, and you'll make space for magic to flow and for you to grow.

Wind Spell to Dispel Confusion and Summon Clarity

When you need it most, thinking clearly can be the most difficult thing to do. It's time to ask Air for help. Magic travels on the winds that blow through all of Creation, clearing away confusion. Cast this spell to banish uncertainty and give yourself clarity.

You'll need

~   A windy day

Cast your spell

1. Go outside to wherever the wind is blowing wildly.

2. Feel the wind on your skin, feel your clothes tugging and flapping against your body, feel your hair being lifted and tousled.

3. Invite the wind to work with you.

4. Ask it to clear your mind, to blow away your confusion and mental clutter.

5. Breathe deeply.

6. Feel the wind entering your body, your mind, your spirit.

7. Feel the wind, breathe deep, and let go!

8. Feel the openness and transparency of your mind.

9. Look around you: Clouds are flying overhead, trees are swaying, birds flying. Everything is moving. Your sight, your mind, your thinking are as clear as the Air.

10. Thank the wind.

11. Your spell is cast.

Act in accord

Return home and write down what you know to be true.

Eagle's View Spell for a New Perspective

There are times when you need to see things from a fresh perspective, whether it's a conflict with yourself or someone else, or you're feeling uncertain, or you're just not sure what the best way forward might be.

This spell works with the spirits of wise birds to give you a fresh point of view. Let them lift you high enough to see the big picture.

You'll need

~ A feather (that you found during your walks through Nature)

~ A white candle

~ Some sandalwood incense—a stick, or powder with incense charcoal

~ A censer

~ Matches

~ Pen and paper, or your journal

Cast your spell

1. Lower the lights and light the candle.

2. Light the incense stick or the charcoal and put a teaspoon of the powdered incense on it.

3. Sit comfortably. Breathe. Quiet your mind and body.

4. Enjoy the calming effect of the incense smoke.

5. Call Eagle, Hawk, or Owl to work with you.

6. Close your eyes. Hold the feather. Feel your guide arriving.

7. Envision yourself with your Bird, flying high above the ground, far from all the problems, responsibilities, and sources of stress.

8. Feel how good it is to be free and far from your worries.

9. As you're flying, ask yourself what you'll care about in a month, a year, five years from now. What's really important to you?

10. See that truly important thing beneath you. Drop gently down until you see it clearly. Stand in front of it, free from anxiety and fully present with what matters.

11. Open your eyes.

12. Add another teaspoon of incense to the charcoal.

13. Write down what matters in your journal.

14. Write down and repeat this Affirming Spell:

> *I let go of worry*
> *and worry lets go of me.*
> *I embrace what matters most*
> *and what matters most gives me hope!*

15. Now that you know what matters to you, it will be easier to let go of the things that don't matter and easier to give yourself to the things that do.

16. Your spell is cast!

Act in accord

The next time something that doesn't matter causes you stress, repeat:

> *I let go of worry, and worry lets go of me.*
> *I embrace what matters most,*
> *and what matters most gives me hope.*

Divination Spell for Guidance

Divination enables you to speak with the Sacred whenever you need guidance, whether it's simply for the day ahead or a life-changing decision. Cast this divination spell for guidance from a compassionate source that always has your best interests at heart.

You'll need

~ Your favorite method of divination, or the Library Angel (*page 25*)

~ Your journal

~ A pen

~ A candle

Cast your spell

1. Light the candle.

2. Hold your method of divination to your heart and ask the Sacred to speak to you.

3. Ask simply:

   Divine who watches over me, what do I need to know?

4. Or ask more specifically:

> *Divine who watches over me, what do I need to*
> *know about [specific issue or concern].*

5. Shuffle, shake, toss, let the book fall open to the answer.

6. Study the message you've received. Read, reflect, interpret. Consider how you can take the advice.

7. Write in your journal about the message and its meaning for you.

8. Thank the Divine for its guidance. Blow out the candle.

Act in accord

Take the advice you've received.

Quick Spell for the Power to Change

Even when you know it's time, it can feel difficult to muster the energy you need to change yourself or your circumstances. Cast this quick, potent spell to release your past and unleash your power to move on!

You'll need

~ An empty jar with a lid

~ Dried peas, corn, beans, or rice

Cast your spell

If you can, work outdoors.

1. Fill your jar a quarter full with the dried peas, corn, beans, or rice.

2. Envision what you need to change.

3. Tighten the lid.

4. Rattle, dance, and spin *widdershins* (opposite the direction of the Sun's "movement.")

5. Make a great noise and release the past!

6. When you feel the shift, stop rattling. Turn and face the opposite direction.

7. Rattle, dance, and spin *deosil* (the direction of the Sun's "movement.")

8. Stir the Air with the energy of your soul vibrating to its purpose.

9. When you feel the shift, release your magic with a final, loud "Huzzzzzah!"

10. Offer the contents of your rattle to Mother Earth with thanks.

Act in accord

Take the necessary actions to change what you need to. Leave the past behind you. Move into the future you are creating.

SPELLS FOR INSPIRATION, CREATIVITY, AND PURPOSE

~

There are times when it can be difficult to see your gifts, to recognize your purpose, to trust that the world needs what you alone can create. Cast these spells and remember that you are here for reasons that will make your heart sing and make the world a better place.

Quick Spell for Inspiration

Sometimes all you need is a flash of inspiration, a bit of brilliance, a playful nudge from your Muse to awaken your creativity. This sensory spell will stimulate your imagination with perfumed magic.

You'll need

~ An Inspiration Oil, which is equal parts:

   ▫ Mastic essential oil

   ▫ Cinnamon essential oil

   ▫ Myrrh essential oil

~ A little bottle

~ A funnel

Cast your spell

~ Mix the three oils to your liking.

~ Sniff, mix, swirl, sniff. Let the magic travel through your happy nose and stir your imagination.

~ When your nose knows your oil is just right, anoint your forehead with a potent dot of inspiration.

~ Feel your mind clear, your concentration focus, and your creativity begin to flow.

~ Your spell is cast. The magic is manifesting.

Muse Spell for Creativity

You are a creative person. There is a gift of expression that is uniquely your own, a thing that gives you joy in the doing. But there may be times when you doubt, dawdle, or find yourself stuck in the mud. How do you find the divine, creative spark within you?

This spell invokes the aid and inspiration of one of the Muses, the Greek Goddesses who were the sacred source of poetry, songs, dance, stories, and the sciences.

Invoke your Muse and cast this spell of artistic conjuring to get your creative juices flowing.

You'll need

~   A candle in whatever color speaks to you

~   Pen and paper

~   A Muse (*see page 152*)

~   An altar to your Muse

~   Whatever you feel you need to encourage your creativity

~   Something to wear

Preparation

~ Allow your intuition to help you find your Muse from this list:

- Calliope, Muse of Eloquence and Heroic Poetry

- Erato, Muse of Love or Erotic Poetry

- Polymnia, Muse of Sacred Poetry (hymns)

- Terpsichore, Muse of the Dance

- Thalia, Muse of Comedy

- Clio, Muse of History

- Euterpe, Muse of Music, Song, and Lyric Poetry

- Melpomene, Muse of Tragedy

- Urania, Muse of Astronomy

~ Read, listen, look, stimulate your creativity with the creativity of others.

~ Surround yourself with scents, statues, colors, objects of Nature, artwork, books, music, beauty, and examples of creativity to inspire yours.

~ Purify yourself and your space.

~ Clear your desk, your workspace, your studio, your creative space. If you don't have one, create one—even a dedicated corner of your bedroom or living room will do, as long as it's set up and ready for when you are.

~ Create an altar for your Muse, using your creativity.

Cast your spell

1. Focus on your intention to create.

2. Set the mood—a good one helps creativity! Put on music that makes you happy. Light incense you like, or use your quick Inspiration Oil (*see previous spell*).

3. Put on your creativity hat, shirt, slippers, and/or jewelry to get the energies flowing. Charge them with this intention, declaring that they are your creativity clothing/jewelry.

4. Write and read aloud an invocation/honoring of your Muse. Ask them for their help. If you prefer, you could use this brief invocation inspired by Homer's *Odyssey*:

> *Divine Muse, Goddess, inspire my*
> *spirit and sustain my effort…*

5. Light your candle.

6. Doodle, scribble, stream your consciousness, listen to the music, play… it doesn't matter what or how you create, just show up.

7. Don't judge yourself or what you've done. It's all good.

8. Thank your Muse.

9. Blow out the candle to set and end the spell.

Act in accord

Tomorrow, cast the spell again and continue your creative project where you left off…

Devote time to it and make it sacred. Make being creative a ritual, something you do consistently. As your creativity starts flowing, let it expand into the rest of your life, your work, your home…

Pay attention when you spend time in Nature and when you dream, as it is then that your unconscious brings you creative gifts from the deep sea of your soul. Keep a pad with you to write things down.

Honor your Muse. Commit yourself to creating what you love and your Muse will bless you.

Spell to Stop Procrastinating and Make That Deadline!

File your taxes, get the job done, deliver the project! Deadlines can trigger paralysis, procrastination, and all sorts of clever avoidance. Or you can cast this daily spell to power through to that finish line like Abebe Bikila winning the Olympic marathon in his bare feet. A deadline isn't about what has to be done, it's about *you* doing it.

You'll need

~ A paper calendar

~ A thick red pen

~ A vow to yourself

Cast your spell

1. Set your intention. Name your task.

2. Circle the deadline on the calendar; write what you have to do. Draw balloons, flowers, flames, happy faces, stuff that reminds you how great it will feel to accomplish your goal.

3. Center yourself.

4. Face East and say:

> *Spirits of Air, bless me with clarity.*
> *Help me to think and express myself clearly.*

5. Face South (or North in the Southern Hemisphere) and say:

> *Spirits of Fire, bless me with energy.*
> *Give me determination and drive to reach my deadline.*

6. Face West and say:

> *Spirits of Water, bless me with love and self-care.*
> *Let worry, self-doubt, and stress flow away and*
> *let hope, confidence, and optimism flow in.*

7. Face North (or South in the Southern Hemisphere) and say:

> *Spirits of Earth, bless me with strength and stamina.*
> *Help me to work well and accomplish my goal in time.*

8. Stand at the center of yourself and say:

> *Spirit, keep me centered and help me*
> *accomplish my goal in time!*

9. Make a vow to yourself that you will make your deadline. Say aloud, three times, with commitment:

> *Yes, I can and I will!*

10. See yourself getting it done. Feel how good it will be to complete this task.

11. Your spell is cast. Go straight to work.

Act in accord

Clear the time and make your work sacred. Quickly center yourself every day before you work. Inertia will fade and momentum will build and carry you along.

When you've made your deadline, declare, three times: "I did it!" Write it on your calendar in big red letters. Congratulate yourself and celebrate. Next time will be easier because *yes, you can!*

Empowering Good Habits Spell

Sometimes it can seem so hard to create a new habit, even when it's something you want to do. Stop struggling and start celebrating with this spell that will literally change your brain and make your new habit fun. Cast this spell and take steps to be healthier and happier with a new, fun, good habit.

You'll need

~   All you need is yourself

Cast your spell

1.   Set your intention. What's your new habit for living well?

2.   Do it, whatever it is. It doesn't have to be perfectly done, or take long. Just do it!

3.   When you're done, celebrate in a way that makes you feel happy, empowered, and successful. Keep it simple and real. For example, say out loud, like you mean it:

   I did it and I'm amazing! I've got the magic and it's working!

4.   Do something physical that reinforces that good feeling: Applaud yourself. Do the Snoopy dance. *Smile!* That will set your spell and send it into high gear!

Act in accord

Celebrate every time you've completed your good habit. The more you give yourself over to the positive emotions you're generating and reinforcing, the faster your habit will take hold.

Quick Spell for a Clear Direction

When daily life seems to have you running in circles instead of fulfilling your dreams and manifesting your purpose, it's time to ask the Universe to guide you. Cast this spell for a clear direction, but be willing to put down your map and trust the adventure that your life is meant to be.

You'll need

~   5 minutes

Preparation

~   If you want, create a Clear Direction Incense to burn or a Clear Direction Potion to carry wrapped in a green fabric bundle tied with green cord from equal parts of the following:

   ▢   Bay

   ▢   Cayenne

   ▢   Coriander

- ▢ Frankincense

- ▢ Juniper

- ▢ Mugwort

- ▢ Myrrh

- ▢ Oregano

- ▢ Peppermint

Cast your spell

1. Hold your Clear Direction Potion in your hand, or light your Clear Direction Incense.

2. Face East, close your eyes, stretch out your arms, and turn slowly clockwise.

3. Turn inward. Where is it you wish to go?

4. Spin slowly until your heart says, "Stop!"

5. Open your eyes and take a step in the direction your heart has chosen.

6. Your spell has begun.

Act in accord

Work magically with the element of the direction your heart has chosen for the next lunar cycle. Carry your Clear Direction Potion with you as you travel forward and trust that you are supported with every step you take.

Spiral Spell to Find Your Purpose

There are times when life feels like a maze and your goals, your dreams, your purpose seem as far away as the Moon. But inside you, the sacred spiral of your DNA holds the pattern of your destiny, the purpose of your life. If you can see it, you can be it. Let this spell help you see the magic you were born to manifest.

You'll need

Some or all of:

~ A snail's shell

~ A nautilus shell

~ A sunflower

~ A pine cone

~ A pineapple

~ A cauliflower

~ A red cabbage cut in half

~ A cactus

~ A picture of a hurricane

~ A picture of a galaxy

~ A picture of the horns of a goat

~ A picture of a fern before it opens

~ Your fingerprint

~ A mirror

~ A divination tool

~ Your journal

~ An altar

Cast your spell

1. Be clear in your intention to see, know, and manifest your purpose.

2. Cast your circle.

3. Place the spirals you've collected on your altar or in front of you.

4. Pick them up, turn them around, feel their texture and their patterns beneath your fingertips. Look carefully at their spiral patterns. They are objects of power embodying magic and revealing the divine pattern of life.

5. Look at your fingerprint. Look in the mirror.

6. Perform a Spiral Dance:

   ▫ Ask one of the objects of power to work with you.

   ▫ Hold it to your heart, receive its blessing.

   ▫ Holding it, slowly begin to move counterclockwise outward from your altar in an ever-widening spiral.

   ▫ When you reach the outermost point, hold your power object up to realms of Spirit then down to Mother Earth.

- ▫ Turn in the opposite direction and begin to move clockwise inward in ever-tightening spirals until you reach the altar.

- ▫ Hold your power object to your heart and thank it.

7. Sit and contemplate the spiraling magic of life before you, around you, within you.

8. Using your divination tool, ask the Sacred what you need to see to know and manifest your purpose.

9. *Feel* your purpose within your heart, *feel* your ability to live your purpose in the world. Feel your magic.

10. The first thing that magic changes is you: When you find your purpose, you find your strength.

11. Thank Spirit. Thank Mother Earth.

12. Close your circle.

Act in accord

Keep these spirals of life in places of respect, eating what's edible.

Work with your object of power to continue to manifest your purpose with vision and strength.

Knot Spell for Determination

Knot magic is a very old practice that can be used for many purposes. Here is an old, very potent way of working it from my first *Grimoire*, within a spell to fortify your determination.

You'll need

~ A red cord 13 inches (33 cm) long. (Use a cord of whatever color is appropriate for other goals.)

Cast your spell

1. Envision yourself feeling and acting with determination.

2. Compose a rhyming spell for it. You might say:

   Here with determination I stand,
   my life created at my command.

3. Hold the cord in your hands and concentrate as you make a knot at one end.

4. Chant your spell as you make the knot. You'll feel it working in your body, psyche, and soul each time you pull the cord tight into a knot, the energy radiating through you and out into Creation.

5. Make a second knot at the other end.

6. For a "light" or quick spell, make a knot in the center; a total of three knots:

7. For a strong spell (especially for protection or to bind negativity), make nine knots, following the knotting pattern back and forth:

8. With each knot, feel your determination growing stronger.

9. When you tie the last knot, feel your determination flowing through you.

10. Set your spell by declaring: "So mote it be!"

Act in accord

Keep your cord somewhere safe, or with you, until your determination has borne fruit or your spell's purpose manifests.

To reinforce your spell, touch each knot in the order in which you tied them and chant or repeat your spell silently.

When your spell has manifested, or to undo the spell, work from the center out, untying the knots in reverse order and releasing the spell as you go.

Celebrate Your Success Spell

If you're like me, you probably tend to overlook your own accomplishments, assuming they're simply what's expected of you as you move on to the next task. It's time to recognize and honor what you've achieved and give yourself the respect and congratulations you've earned. Cast this spell to celebrate your success!

You'll need

~ An altar of your achievements

~ Your favorite flowers

~ A candle in your favorite color

~ Something you love to wear

~ Something delicious to eat and drink

~ Music you love

Preparation

~ Set up your altar, filled with examples, photos, objects, and symbols of what you've created or accomplished—pictures of yourself or your children, books you've written, diplomas and honors you've been awarded, the first dollar you earned, your artwork, craftwork, volunteer work, spiritual practices, or athletic achievements (like the sneakers you wore in a marathon).

~   Put on your party duds.

~   Turn on the music.

Cast your spell

1. Go to your altar. Look at what you've accomplished. Take your time and *really* take it in. It's kind of amazing, isn't it?

2. Uncork the champagne or whatever you want to drink. Toast yourself, and declare out loud *and loud*:

> *I did it! Yes, I did! I did it!*
> *I did that, and that, and that!*
> *Because: Yes, I can! And I have!*
> *And I will again!*
> *So mote it be!*

3. Enjoy yourself. You deserve it!

4. Your spell is cast.

Act in accord

The next time you accomplish something, take the time to honor your success and celebrate, in a meaningful, even if small, way.

Spells for Protection, Strength, and Courage

~

We live in a time of difficult global challenges, and fear, worry, and feeling vulnerable can be reasonable reactions to unreasonable circumstances. Life is also full of personal test and trials, but when you face them, you'll discover that you're stronger than you thought. Here are spells to summon the life-protecting, loving, wondrous power that you are.

Quick Sphere of Protection Spell

Should you ever need it, it's important to have the power to protect yourself. It's also helpful to be able to shield yourself from life's little aggravations, unintended accidents, and negative energies, whether they're a grouchy boss or an overpacked subway, an online troll or an autocratic tyrant. Wrap yourself in a sphere of light with this Protection Spell to stay calm, secure, and safe.

Cast your spell

1. Set your intention (with determination) to surround yourself with impenetrable protection.

2. Place your hands over your stomach. Feel the energy, heat, power. Visualize a sphere of light in the center of your stomach.

3. Clap your hands *hard*, stretch your arms out palms outward and send the sphere out and all around you, covering you completely.

4. Feel the energy flowing through your palms around you, in front of and behind you, above and below you.

5. Feel the sphere of energy, power, and protection surrounding you.

6. Declare: "I'm safe. I'm protected. I'm secure."

7. If you are in a public space, visualize the energy being sent out from your center.

8. When you don't need the Protection Sphere anymore, reach out and grasp it with both hands and pull it back into your stomach. Or see yourself doing it.

Charm for Protection from Negative Energies

This is a very old spell from an English *Grimoire* to create a protective charm against "psychic attack," a rather dramatic term for today's negative energies. I've included substitutes that are easier to get. Cast whenever you need that extra bit of protection.

You'll need

~ A small pouch

~ An amber bead and a jet bead

~ Elderflowers (or elderberries)

~ Nettle (garlic)

~ Blood root (coriander)

~ Mandrake (tobacco)

~ Mistletoe (mint or sage)

~ Low John (galangal root or ginger)

Cast your spell

1. Cast your circle.

2. Set your intention to protect yourself against negative energies.

3. Take the pouch and put the items into it to make the charm. Breathe your intention to be safe and secure into the Protection Pouch.

4. Bless it by drawing a pentagram over the Protection Pouch with your dominant hand.

5. Hang the charm over the door or carry it with you.

6. Your spell is cast!

Putting elderflowers into each corner of the room is also very effective. Sweep them away periodically and lay down a fresh batch.

Boundary Spell

Caring for others is part of being a good and happy human. But whether you're a professional caregiver or simply living your life as a friend and family member, you need to have healthy boundaries. And daily life—at work, at the grocery store, at the gas station—can confront you with behavior that can try your patience and challenge your love for humanity. This is a spell to erect and reinforce healthy boundaries to keep negative energies out and to protect and preserve your peace of mind, energy, and well-being. It's a spell of empowering self-care.

You'll need

~ A handful of salt

~ If you wish, a small amber bottle, small funnel, and a powerful Boundary Protection Oil made with:

  ▫ 2 tablespoons of jojoba oil

  ▫ 5 drops each of the essential oils of cedar, cinnamon, geranium, peppermint, and rue

  ▫ A pinch of ground rosemary

Preparation

~ Create your Boundary Protection Oil:

  ▫ Pour the oils into a small amber bottle.

  ▫ Close and shake the bottle. Smell and adjust the oil by carefully adding small amounts of the scents you prefer until you find it pleasing.

  ▫ Shake the bottle again feeling the energy of the oils combining.

~ Charge the oil with your power and intention of setting protective boundaries around yourself.

Cast your spell

1. Cast a circle around yourself, sprinkling salt as you go. Feel the circle forming a boundary all around you, above and below you, keeping any negative energy outside and your positive energy, peacefulness, calm, and confidence inside you.

2. Say:

> *I conjure the power around and within.*
> *Shield and protect me from all intrusion.*

3. Dab a drop of your Boundary Protection Oil on your finger and touch your third eye, your throat, heart, stomach, root chakra, and wrists. (Do *not* touch your eyes.)

4. Take three deep breaths, inhaling the perfume and power of the oil that is expanding the boundaries that protect you from intrusion, confusion, or depletion.

5. When you feel your boundaries are securely set, close your circle.

Act in accord

Wear your Boundary Protection Oil whenever you feel intruded upon, silently repeating your spell as you reinforce a strong boundary around yourself. You can also keep a bit of salt in your pocket.

Distance yourself from people who drain your energies. Saying "No, sorry, I can't," can be an appropriate boundary spell.

And let your gut guide you—if your intuition says stay away, do it.

Quick Return to Sender Spell

This is old magic, and my preferred technique, of effortlessly refusing delivery of negative energies. No need to engage or to waste precious time, emotions, or energy—just cast this spell to return the negativity whence it came and get on with living well.

You'll need

~ A small mirror (a compact mirror is excellent as it can sit upright), or a Witch's Ball, which is a small ornament covered in tiny mirrors

Cast your spell

1. Place your mirror facing away from you and toward whoever or whatever is sending negativity your way.

2. Or hang the Witch's Ball (originally said to keep Witches away, but we know the real magic) in a window or doorway to bounce the negativity back to the sender.

3. Your spell is cast. Get on with living well.

Peace and Protection Potion

Having to protect yourself can feel unsettling. This little potion and the herbs and oils from which it is made can help you maintain your equilibrium and sense of well-being.

You'll need

~   4 parts (p) lavender

~   3 p basil

~   3 p thyme

~   2 p frankincense

~   2 p vervain

~   A pinch of rue

~   A pinch of benzoin

~   A few drops of the essential oils of jasmine and bergamot

Cast your spell

1.   See yourself safe, peaceful, and protected.

2.   Mix your potion as you envision your well-being.

3.   Wrap it in blue fabric tied with blue ribbon, or a cotton handkerchief, or fill a muslin bag.

4.   Inhale its perfume and carry it with you.

5. Your spell is cast!

The potion also works as a wonderful peace and protection bath.

Quick Spell for Warrior's Courage

Thyme is an ancient herb, a gift of strength from Mother Earth, deeply respected for its power to protect and give courage. Warriors of ancient Greece burned it in the temples. Roman soldiers bathed in Waters infused with it. English fighters stuffed it in their boots when they charged into battle and wore it as a badge of honor on their chests. Cast this spell for thyme to lend you its potent magic when you need an extra bit of courage.

You'll need

~   A bit of thyme

Cast your spell

1. Ask the thyme, plant of power, for its help.

2. Put a bit of thyme in your shoes and your pockets.

3. As you do, say, with conviction:

If I'm afraid then I must
turn fear to courage and doubt to trust!

4. Thank the thyme for lending you its power. Thank Mother Earth for her support.

5. Your spell is cast—you've got this!

Act in accord

Remember the trick: Feel your fear and act anyway. Courage is your reward.

Bear's Heart Spell for Courage Under Pressure

There are times when you must defend what's right. The secret of this magic is that when you serve something greater than yourself, it will make you greater than you are. You'll discover that you have the power to do what's right, even if it seems to put you on the losing side. When you face the worst, cast this spell for Bear's courage and it will bring out your own.

You'll need

~   To create an altar for Bear

~   The ingredients for a Bear's Heart Potion:

    ▫   Ground bayberry (or English bog myrtle)

    ▫   Ground buckeye

- ▢ 1 bay leaf

- ▢ Some basil

- ▢ 5 datura seeds (also called moonflower, thornapple, jimson weed or devil's trumpet; do not eat these, as they can be dangerous) or substitute white carnation

- ▢ 3 drops of raw honey or a piece of honeycomb

~ A stone and bit of soil from where you live or your place of power

~ A small leather pouch

Cast your spell

1. Set your intention to honor Bear and invoke her help in finding your courage.

2. Mix the ingredients together, add the stone and the soil, and put them in the pouch.

3. Ground yourself. Feel the energy of Mother Earth, Mother Bear, coming to you to give you courage.

4. Charge your Bear's Heart Potion, holding it to your heart.

5. Thank Mother Earth, Mother Bear.

6. Your spell is cast.

Act in accord

Carry your potion with you when you need Bear's magic. Return it to Mother Earth when you no longer need it.

SPELLS FOR
SELF-AWARENESS
AND SERENITY

*Self-awareness is the beginning of self-acceptance,
inner peace, and the power to change. These
spells will help you see yourself clearly and with
compassion and trust that you are never alone—the
magic and support you need are ever present. That
support can include therapeutic and medical care
that these spells don't replace, but complement.*

Spell for Dis-Spelling Social Anxiety

It's not unusual to feel uncomfortable in unfamiliar social situations. But what if you're experiencing anxiety that keeps you from going out or interacting with people? Or what if you just feel awkward and uncomfortable? A spell can be a wonderful way to dis-spell your anxiety—it can literally change the way you're thinking and so change the way you're acting and reacting.

This is a slow, easy, step-by-step spell to ease yourself out of isolation and into greater comfort and connection.

You'll need

~ Pen and paper

~ Scotch tape

~ A pink candle

~ Matches

Cast your spell

1. Set your intention to feel less anxious.

2. Cast a simple circle around yourself.

3. Ask the spirits of Air to help you think clearly.

4. Ask the spirits of Fire to give you courage.

5. Ask the spirits of Water to keep you calm.

6. Ask the spirits of Earth to keep your body grounded.

7. Sit in the center of your circle. Light the candle.

8. Remind yourself that the first thing magic changes is you.

9. Take some deep, calming breaths.

10. Think about being in a social situation that causes you anxiety.

11. Write your negative beliefs about yourself or others—e.g. "I'm boring, I'm unlikeable, people are only nice because they want something from me"—on the piece of paper.

12. Declare your readiness to release that way of thinking and feeling.

13. Tear the paper into large pieces and feel the anxious thoughts and feelings leaving you.

14. Breathe. Feel your clarity, courage, calmness, and groundedness.

15. Turn the torn pieces of paper written sides down.

16. Now ask yourself: "How can I approach the situation differently? Have I been in a social setting in which I felt good about myself or in which others surprised me? Can I bring my awareness to the hidden helpers wherever I am—a friend in the room, a pretty piece of artwork that makes me feel good, a plant or a tree, or even a friendly spirit? How would I like to talk to myself instead?"

17. Write your answers on the papers. Tape them back together.

18. Feel how different the energy is on your paper and in your body.

19. Affirm that you are replacing your negative script with a positive one.

20. Write a simple Affirming Spell, for example:

I am safe.
I belong.
In myself, I stand strong.

21. Read it aloud, repeating until it becomes a chant.

22. Place your hands over your heart and feel the energy flowing into you.

23. Feel your spell working within you.

24. When you're ready, thank the elements for their blessing.

25. Blow out your candle.

26. Close your circle.

27. Get some rest.

Act in accord

Cross out the old script. Keep your new script face up and your Affirming Spell somewhere safe, like your journal, or stick it under a plant you care for, so when you're caring for the plant, you're growing those things inside yourself.

Reread it whenever you need reminding of it. The next time you're in a social situation, when the negative self-talk starts, pause. Remember your intention to talk to yourself in the new way. Repeat your Affirming Spell to yourself. Feel the confident voice inside you growing and your anxiety diminishing. Commit that new feeling to memory. Smile. The magic is working. You're changing.

Self-Acceptance Spell

Learn the lessons from your past and you'll find the magic to accept yourself as you are now, to see yourself with kindness, with your strengths *and* your weaknesses. From this place of self-acceptance, you can decide how to take better care of yourself, what you want or need to change, and what steps to take to make those changes. This is a gentle spell for self-acceptance.

You'll need

~   An altar or small table to hold an upright mirror

~   A candle

~   Your journal

~   Pen and paper

~   A sandalwood incense stick or powder with incense charcoal

~   A censer

~   Matches

Cast your spell

1.   Cast your circle.

2.   Light your incense.

3.   Put the candle in front of your mirror. Light it.

4. In your journal, write your intention to accept yourself as you are.

5. Reflect on what you think of as mistakes, but write about them as opportunities to learn. Answer these three questions:

   ▢ What did I learn?

   ▢ What are the things I do well, including small things?

   ▢ What are my strengths?

6. Write down an Affirming Spell that's meaningful to you. For example:

   I've learned from my past, that's over and done.
   With love and acceptance, my future's begun.

7. Look in the mirror and see the light shining in your eyes.

8. Recite your spell as you look in the mirror.

9. Keep reciting it until you smile at yourself.

10. Vow to be kinder to yourself.

11. Blow out your candle.

12. Your spell is cast.

13. Close your circle.

Act in accord

Ask a trusted friend what they see as your strengths and what they value about you. You're wonderful and wise *because* of who you are just as you are. Be kind to yourself.

Solar Blast Spell for When You're Feeling SAD

When Winter comes and the Sun goes, bears hibernate, fish sleep, trees slumber. Things naturally slow down to rest, and you should too, but work has to be done. Seasonal Affective Disorder is a real thing, especially for women whose hormones are affected by the lack of sunlight, and who can feel depressed, sluggish, and unable to concentrate. And even if you're always tired, it can be hard to sleep.

This is an old-school, big-scale Solar Blast Spell for Winter's light deprivation. Keep yourself charged by breaking it into smaller, regularly repeated Solar Spells until Spring returns, along with your natural energy!

The best time to cast this is during Winter when the Sun is high in the sky, but do it when you need it.

You'll need

~   Something yellow or orange to wear

~   Your altar

~   A yellow or orange cloth

~   A yellow or orange seven-day pillar candle

~   A small knife

~   Sun Oil: Equal parts frankincense and myrrh oils

~ Solar Incense: Frankincense and myrrh, with 3 drops of the Sun Oil

~ Incense charcoal and matches

~ Yellow and orange flower petals

~ Music that makes you happy

~ A bowl

~ Honey

~ Something good to eat

~ An image of the Sun, or a solar deity (optional)

Preparation

~ Turn the music on.

~ Set up your Solar Blast altar.

~ Mix your oil.

~ Thank the herbs and mix your incense.

Cast your spell

1. Cast your circle.

2. Light the charcoal and put a teaspoon of the Solar Incense on it to burn.

3. Set your intention to charge yourself with positive, sunny, fiery energy. See yourself feeling better, more enthusiastic, more energetic.

4. Invoke the power of the Sun.

5. Hold the candle to your heart and state your intention:

> *Help me feel the light shining within me,*
> *feel the Fire burning bright within me.*

6. Prepare your Solar Blast Candle:

    ▫ Carve the candle with a symbol of the Sun as a sigil for feeling re-energized.

    ▫ Oil the candle with your Sun Oil, from wick to end, drawing the power of the Sun and Fire toward yourself as you do so.

    ▫ Enjoy the fragrance and feel yourself being energized.

    ▫ Put the flower petals in the bowl.

    ▫ Put the candle in the bowl on the petals.

    ▫ Drip the honey on the candle and the petals.

    ▫ Taste the honey. Remember Spring and Summer will come again with all their sweetness.

7. Light the candle. Feel your intention turning into energy as you strike the match and light the wick.

8. Cup your hands around the candle flame and bring the light into your heart. Feel it burning within you.

9. Chant the spell:

> *Flame of life returning,*
> *within me brightly burning!*

10. Dance. Feel the Fire burning within you.

11. Before the flame of your energy peaks, give thanks to the Sun, to the light within yourself, to your body and your spirit.

12. Ground yourself by eating what you've prepared. Drink some Water. Taste the honey. Feel your energy flowing through you.

13. Close your circle.

Act in accord—the spell continues...

~ Put the candle someplace safe and let it burn for the next seven days until the spell is done.

~ Every day, spend a few minutes in front of it.

~ Bring the flame into your heart, your mind, your solar plexus.

~ Chant: "Flame of life returning, within me brightly burning!"

~ When the candle has burned down and the spell is done, thank the Sun for the life it gives you and Mother Earth.

Act in accord with practical magic for light-deprived self-care

~ Go outside every day to greet the Sun, even if it's cloudy. Congratulate yourself *out loud* and *with enthusiasm* for getting outside. Just ten minutes of light on your retina makes a real difference.

~ Put full-spectrum light bulbs in all your lamps and get a light box: Starting light therapy as Fall begins can help stave off SAD symptoms.

~ Wear bright colors from the solar end of the spectrum like red, orange, yellow, and pink.

~ Eat well, choosing foods that release energy slowly and that will help to keep your sugar levels steady, like non-starchy vegetables such as cauliflower, broccoli, and spinach, brown rice, oats, cereals, nuts, and seeds.

Spell for a Spark of Energy in the Dark of Depression

Depression can make the simplest tasks feel impossible. Just getting out of bed and taking a shower can zap all the energy you have for the day. Here is a spell for a spark to light your way out of the dark of depression and back to life.

You'll need

~ A white candle

~ Matches

~ Pen and paper

~ An object of power

Cast your spell

1. Cast your circle.

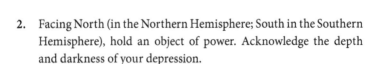

2. Facing North (in the Northern Hemisphere; South in the Southern Hemisphere), hold an object of power. Acknowledge the depth and darkness of your depression.

3. Facing South (in the Northern Hemisphere; North in the Southern Hemisphere), light the candle and honor the powers of Fire. Ask them to awaken the spark of Fire within you.

4. Cup your hands behind the flame and bring it into your heart and solar plexus.

5. Allow yourself to feel the small flame within you. Trust what you sense, see, experience.

6. The light, the heat, the power of the candle is the light, the heat, the power of the flame you find within you.

7. Welcome this spark of life force, this energy inside you, no matter its size. Feel it shine in the darkness.

8. Write one small task you would like to accomplish on your piece of paper.

9. Set your candle atop the piece of paper to illuminate the task.

10. Bring your attention back to the flame inside you and know that you will have this energy to complete the task.

11. Thank the powers of Fire.

12. Feel proud of your accomplishment. Use your pride to stoke the flame inside. Congratulate yourself out loud, knowing that your words have power: "I found my Fire!"

13. Blow out the candle.

14. Close your circle.

Act in accord

Repeat as you need to.

When you're ready, cast the spells for One Small Thing (*see below*), and remember, don't overwhelm yourself with everything at once. All you need is one small spark, one small thing at a time. And each thing you do is a success to be celebrated!

Spells to Overcome Inertia with One Small Thing

There are days when it's hard just to get out of bed. It could be the debilitating blues or the mean reds. This is a spell for one small thing, because one small thing can make a world of difference. It can ease the emotional paralysis, stop the negative ruminating, relieve your resistance one small step at a time. And remember, you don't have to do it on your own—consult a therapist, mental health specialist, or doctor for the help you need.

You'll need

~   A white candle

~   Pen and paper

~   Peppermint soap

~   Clothes

~ Shoes

~ A friend's phone number

Preparation

~ Take a shower using the peppermint soap (don't get it in your eyes).

~ Get dressed.

Here are four small spells to choose from. Pick the easiest one.

"One Small Thing" Spell

1. Light the white candle.

2. Take a few breaths.

3. Read your spell:

> *I have just one thing to do today:*
> *Take care of myself in one small way.*

4. Repeat until you feel a small shift inside. You can also repeat this when you're doing your One Small Thing.

5. Blow out your candle.

Act in accord

Pick One Small Thing and do it.

Next week, pick One Small Thing and do it.

Look Around Spell

1. Go outside. Take a walk. Look up, look around, look at Nature.

2. Ask Nature to show you something that will help you see yourself with more kindness, acceptance, hope.

Happy Memory Spell

1. When a bad memory feels overwhelming, remind yourself of a happy one.

2. Visualize yourself in that happy memory. Counter the negative with a dose of positive.

Feed the Good Wolf Talisman Spell

When the loop of annihilating beliefs about yourself starts playing, replace it with positive beliefs:

1. Write a list of your positive qualities and accomplishments.

2. Read it, fold it up, and put it in your wallet or pocket. You've created a Good Wolf talisman of positive change. Read it when the Bad Wolf starts howling. Remember, the one you feed is the one that wins.

Something Fun Spell

1. Call a friend and do something together that you enjoy.

Serenity Spell

We all experience pain, grief, sorrow, or discouragement. We have to deal with things we can't change. But when we have little or no control over a bad situation, we can control how we respond. And when the negative tape loop runs in our ruminating brains, there are ways to change the tape. Cast this spell for serenity, courage, wisdom, and, yes, joy.

You'll need

~ A white candle

~ Sandalwood oil

~ Your journal and a pen

Cast your spell

1. Set your intention to accept the things you cannot change and to change the things you can.

2. Put some of the sandalwood oil on your fingertip and anoint the candle downward from the wick to the base (*see page 120 for the candle anointing diagram*).

3. Put a drop on your third eye and your heart.

4. Light the candle.

5. Take several deep, calming breaths.

6. Recite the Serenity Prayer (below) as your spell, invoking the Higher Power, Goddess, God, Spirit, Source, Creator, Mother Earth, Divine in whatever terms are meaningful to you:

> *[Spirit], grant me the serenity to accept*
> *the things I cannot change,*
> *the courage to change the things I can,*
> *and the wisdom to know the difference,*
> *living one day at a time,*
> *enjoying one moment at a time,*
> *taking this world as it is...*

7. Reflect on accepting what you can't change and changing what you can, reflect on what gives you joy, especially in difficult times, and write about your insights in your journal.

8. When you're done, thank Spirit and close your circle.

Act in accord

If you feel your spells for self-awareness and serenity need an extra boost, please reach out to a therapist or doctor. "Spelling out" your need for help is also a spell!

Spells for Self-Care and Healing

In the midst of a too-busy world, it's important but often difficult to take care of yourself. It can also be daunting to face wounds, injuries, and ailments, whether physical or psychological, but the capacity to heal is innate. Here are some spells for self-care and healing, either for yourself or, simply adapted, for someone or something you care about.

These spells are not offered as medical advice or a replacement for regular medical care, but as a magically empowering, encouraging complement to other therapies and medical care.

Cozy Cup of Tea Spell for Self-Care

There's more magic in brewing a cup of tea than you might think, especially when it comes to self-care and well-being. Cast this spell, relax, reflect, and give yourself the gift of something small and simple that makes you happy.

You'll need

~   Your favorite self-care teas, like chamomile, honey, ginger, lemon, peppermint, green, raspberry leaf, or a magical mix

~   A tea kettle or pot

~   A favorite teacup or mug and spoon

~   Honey, if you like it

Cast your spell

1.   Choose your tea.

2.   Boil the Water and pour it over the tea leaves.

3.   Breathe in the scent and enjoy every sip you take.

4.   Your spell is cast.

Act in accord

Do something small and lovely for yourself every day—have your tea, listen to music that makes you calm and happy, play with a furry family member, take a walk. Even with magic, small things make a big difference.

Reading to a Tree Spell to De-Stress

Stress is the default position of modern life—constantly checking likes and follows and messages, rushing to work, watching the news. Cast this spell with a compassionate tree and your sense of peace, calm, and connection will return. Cast regularly and your heart will open and your peacefulness deepen. The tree will like it too.

Human nature is always better in Nature. Combine this spell with the Walking Spell (*page 216*) for maximum magic.

You'll need

~ The poem "The Peace of Wild Things" by Wendell Berry, a poem by Mary Oliver, or another poem you love, copied by hand

~ An offering of Water

~ Time

~ A tree

Cast your spell

1. Use the Walking Spell (*page 216*) to move slowly into the peace of the natural world.

2. Pay attention. Your senses will come alive as you go deeper into Nature.

3. Visit a tree you have a relationship with or allow yourself to be called to one.

4. Place your hands on its trunk. Feel time slow, feel yourself slow.

5. Express your gratitude.

6. Tell the tree you'd like to sit beneath it, lean against it, breathe with it, read to it.

7. Sit, close your eyes, breathe.

8. When you feel calm and quiet, open your eyes.

9. Read the poem to the tree.

10. Feel its response. Enjoy each other's company.

11. When you're ready, thank the tree. Thank your mind for coming to rest, your body for holding your spirit, your heart for beating with love. Thank the poet.

12. Pour your Water offering and head slowly home.

Act in accord

Visit the tree regularly and read new poems to it. You're building a relationship that nourishes both of you.

You may also wish to ground with your back against the tree and cast the Breath of Life Spell (*page 244*).

Spell for Sleeping Well

Sleep cures a world of woes—your body heals, your mind rests, your soul wanders into realms of spirit. Problems find solutions, signs are given, and you awaken renewed and ready for all the possibilities of a new day. But sometimes it can be hard to unwind, let go, turn off your brain. Work this spell for sleeping well. The rest will take care of itself, and you.

You'll need

~ A hot bath

~ 1 cup of Epsom salts

~ ½ cup of lavender

~ 2 handkerchiefs or muslin bags

~ A Sleep Well Potion: Mix 5 teaspoons of raw local honey with a few grains of salt

~ Fresh sheets

~ A quiet, dark bedroom

Preparation

~ Turn off all your electronics.

~ Create the Sleep Well Potion by mixing the honey and salt.

~ Put half the lavender in each handkerchief and knot them.

~ Put fresh sheets on your bed. Turn off your phone.

~ Run a hot tub.

~ Stir in the Epsom salts. Add one of the lavender bundles.

Cast your spell

1. Get into the tub slowly.

2. Soak.

3. When you're relaxed and ready for bed, get out and thank the Water and the lavender.

4. Keep the lights low in your bedroom. Put the second lavender bundle inside your pillow.

5. Get into bed. Put a small amount of the Sleep Well Potion on your tongue. Thank the bees.

6. Close your eyes, breathe slowly, and say this little Bedtime Spell:

> *Sweet dreams, pleasant dreams, and good night,*
> *Tonight I sleep deeply, and all is right.*

7. Turn out the lights and goodnight!

Act in accord

You may dream of bees, ancient messengers between the worlds, spirit allies, guides to the magical garden growing within you and in the worlds all around you. A dancing path of magic awaits you…

Spell to Bless Your Body

You're part of the natural world and, like Nature, your body is full of wisdom, beauty, and magic. Regardless of your gender or gender identity, the shape of your body or what shape it's in, your body is life, with its gifts of pleasure and joy, its instincts, and how it alerts you to what it needs, to what *you* need. You, your body and your spirit are One. Cast this spell to bless and honor your body for its sacred wisdom, gifts, and blessings.

You'll need

~ A mirror

~ A bowl of warm Water

~ 3 tablespoons of sea salt

Preparation

~ Stir the salt into the Water until it has dissolved.

Cast your spell

1. Set your intention to honor your body.

2. Take off your clothes and stand in front of your mirror. Don't inspect, don't judge, don't criticize. Be grateful that you have a body that works hard for you in so many ways.

3. Take your salt Water, from which Life first came, and bless yourself: Wet your fingertip and touch your feet, groin, belly, heart, throat, and third eye.

4. Express your gratitude to your body. You might say:

Thank you, my amazing body, for all
the gifts you give me every day.
I promise to listen to you, to take better care
of you, to do what gives you joy.
Together, we'll grow stronger and
healthier and happier every day.
So mote it be!

5. Smile and give yourself a hug.

6. Your spell is cast.

Act in accord

Get dressed and do something nice and healthy for your body.

Create a doable, appropriate exercise routine—it can be as simple as walking regularly (*see also the Walking Spell on page 216*).

Congratulate yourself and thank your body for its blessings.

Healing Spell

It's impossible to live without injury. Let Mother Earth teach you what Spirit knows—the power to heal yourself is natural and sacred. Every wound can be healed, and every healing empowers you, makes you wiser, kinder, and stronger. Cast your spell and heal yourself. Then you can heal others.

You'll need

~ A tablespoon of yarrow

~ A tablespoon of meadowsweet

~ A tablespoon of chamomile

~ A 5-inch (13-cm) square of blue or white cotton cloth or a white handkerchief

~ A blue ribbon

Cast your spell

1. Set your intention to begin to heal, whether the wound is to body, mind, heart, or soul, to take care of yourself with love and compassion in whatever ways you need to heal.

2. Ask the plants (herbs) to bless you with their healing powers and thank them for helping you.

3. Cup the fabric and fill it with the herbs. Carefully tie it up with three knots in the blue ribbon.

4. As you work, chant the Healing Spell:

> *Feeling, feeling, feeling.*
> *It is love, love, love,*
> *that is healing, healing, healing.*
> *All the past sorrows*
> *are the strength of my tomorrows.*

5. Ground yourself and send the healing energies of Mother Earth into your Healing Potion and whatever needs healing.

6. Hold the potion to your heart and to whatever part of you needs healing. Breathe, relax, and feel the warmth, the energy, the healing power of the plants entering and working with you. Thank them for blessing you with well-being.

7. Declare: "My healing spell is cast! My healing has begun."

Act in accord

Be patient and kind with yourself. Give your spell time to work. Attend to yourself with tenderness and encouragement.

Repeat, or simply chant, as needed.

Consult a good doctor if you need to.

When you feel ready, return the herbs with thanks to Mother Earth.

Quick Healing Spell for Yourself or Another

Use this simple spell when you feel the need for healing or wish to offer healing energy to someone or something else.

You'll need

~ A white or blue candle

~ A small knife

~ Matches

Cast your spell

1. Carve your/their name and the word "healthy" on the candle.

2. Light the candle.

3. Place your hands over your heart and chant the Healing Spell:

> *Feeling, feeling, feeling.*
> *It is love, love, love,*
> *that is healing, healing, healing.*

4. As you chant, envision a radiant bubble of healing energy all around yourself/the person that you/they can absorb as needed.

5. See and feel yourself healthy. See them healthy.

6. Breathe, rest, and put the candle someplace safe to burn down.

Act in accord

It's always good, if possible, to ask someone if they would like you to cast a healing spell for them. Let them know that you are sending them a well of healing love and energy to draw from as they wish or need.

Quick Spell with a Medicine Plant

Plants breathe with us, feed us, teach and heal us. Their lives are intertwined with ours. Plant a medicine plant and it will teach you about itself, about yourself, about how Spirit lives in the world and how you are meant to live in the world. If you listen, it will give you a medicine song. Cast this planting spell and it will bless you.

This is a quick spell that requires no more than five minutes, but should be cast regularly, several times a week.

You'll need

~ A medicine plant like chamomile, echinacea, or yarrow

~ A hand trowel

~ Water

~ 5 minutes

Cast your spell

1. Plant a medicine plant in your garden. Welcome it with joy.

2. Tend it with love.

3. Harvest it with gratitude.

4. Dry it in the Sun.

5. Make a healing potion with it.

6. Listen for the song it will teach you as you work with it.

7. When your healing is done, return your plant helper to Mother Earth with thanks.

Act in accord

Take care of your medicine plant, giving thanks for its help, and take care of yourself.

Spell to Heal a Broken Heart

Water is the element of our feelings. Dive deep beneath any turbulence or troubles and you'll find peace, beauty, and love. Cast this Water spell and feel the love that heals all wounds.

You'll need

~ A white candle

~ 9 drops of rose essential oil

~ Some white roses

~ A bathtub

Cast your spell

1. Cast a circle to hold the healing energies.

2. Set your intention to give yourself the love and support you need to heal.

3. Fill your bathtub with warm Water, the drops of rose oil, and white rose petals.

4. Ask the Water to help you heal. Ask it to dissolve your sadness and heal your broken heart. Ask it to carry away your sorrows and fill you with peace.

5. Light your candle.

6. Get in and soak. Feel the healing, compassionate power of the Water surrounding and embracing you.

7. Cry if you need to. Feel the Water accept your tears. Salt Water is healing.

8. Feel your sorrows dissolving in the Water.

9. Focus on the beauty, softness, and magic of the white rose petals floating in the Water, of the Water itself.

10. Offer your love to the roses and to the Water.

11. Feel the love you are putting into the Water, the love flowing all around and into you. Feel the love you are giving yourself.

12. Feel your heart healing.

13. When you're ready, get out of the tub. Thank the Water and drain the tub. Scoop up the petals and put them in a bowl.

14. Blow out the candle. Close your circle.

Act in accord

Get a good night's rest. In the morning, scatter the petals outside.

Keep taking gentle, patient, loving care of yourself. Healing takes time.

Spell for the Health and Well-Being of a Beloved Animal Companion

We're incredibly blessed that cats and dogs, birds and horses, and countless other amazing creatures have adapted to living with us and are so generous with the love, loyalty, and lessons they offer us. When it comes to their well-being, pay attention to your intuition, because through it they are communicating what they need. Cast this spell to express your love and devotion and to offer a beloved animal companion energy and healing, support and love when they're ill or injured. And consult a vet for the medical help your beloved companion may require.

You'll need

~ A blue candle

~ Matches

~ A small knife

Cast your spell

1. Invite your beloved companion to be with you.

2. Light your candle and invoke the Lady of the Wild Things and the Lord of the Animals:

> *Goddess with your healing touch,*
> *God of the animals' wild domain,*
> *bless [Name of your companion] who I love so much;*
> *cure [Name's] illness, heal his/her pain.*

3. Breathe. Ground yourself and draw the healing energies of Mother Earth into your heart.

4. Quietly chant:

> *Mother Earth, who loves and heals all,*
> *for [Name's] good health to you I call.*
> *God of creatures great and small,*
> *for [Name's] well-being to you I call.*

5. Place your hands over your companion and visualize a slow, gentle stream of love and healing energies flowing to the place that needs healing. If they squirm, get up or move away, simply ask Mother Earth and the God of Animals to bless, heal, and protect them.

6. Give them love and reassurance.

7. When you're ready, thank the Goddess, the God, and Mother Earth.

8. Blow out your candle.

9. Your healing spell is cast.

Act in accord

Listen to your intuition. And have a trusted vet diagnose and advise you on the treatment and care of your beloved companion.

SPELLS WITH
NATURE'S MAGIC

Nature embodies Spirit and so it's full of magic.
Perhaps its greatest magic is that all living things, when
taking good care of themselves in order to be healthy
and happy, are making the world better for all Life.
Pay attention to Nature's magic and you'll discover
your own magic for living well and with wonder.

Walking Spell into Nature's Magic

This simple walking spell has so many blessings: It's great for your mood and mental health, will lower your stress and blood pressure, reduce your anxiety, and help you be more present, mindful, and focused. It will get you into your body and connect you with the body of the natural world, and its life-sustaining, divine magic. Walk into Nature's magic and experience that you're *never* alone.

You'll need

~ A comfortable pair of walking shoes

~ A quiet, natural place to walk in

~ At least 20 minutes

~ A small offering of Water, birdseed, or a piece of fruit

Cast your spell

1. Set your intention to gather your awareness to be present in the moment in a soft, gentle, relaxed way.

2. Walk at a natural pace. Notice your feet touching the ground. Notice the ground beneath your feet. Notice the movements of your body with each step.

3. Walk more slowly. Take in the beauty around you. Breathe. Feel yourself relaxing.

4. What do you hear? Pay attention to the sounds of the natural world—the wind blowing, the leaves rustling, the birds singing. How do you feel?

5. What do you smell? Mother Earth? Pine needles, sage brush, wild roses?

6. How do you feel?

7. Is there a path? Was it made by humans or animals? How does Mother Earth feel beneath your feet? How do you feel being supported by her from below?

8. What do you see? What is the light like? The sky? The terrain?

9. Who is with you? Who is watching you?

10. Just remain open to everything around you. There's nothing you need to do, nothing to fix, nothing to change. Be present in your body, in Nature, aware and walking.

11. Stand still. What do you feel?

12. Move on again. What do you feel?

13. When you come to a welcoming place, sit down. Acknowledge any sense of presence you may be experiencing.

14. Acknowledge the magic that's showing itself to you—everything is taking care of itself and simultaneously making the world in which you are walking better for you and for all life. Witness the beauty.

15. When you're ready, express your gratitude and leave your offering.

16. Walk home slowly, aware of your surroundings, aware of walking.

17. When you're ready to end your walking spell, stand still. Set your spell by thanking Mother Earth for supporting you as you walked your spell.

Act in accord

Let the spell do its work. Allow 24 hours before you write about it or discuss it with anyone.

In the future, you may wish to add to your Walking Spell by asking for a natural power object (*see the following spell*), or the answer to a question, or a sign.

Natural Object of Power Spell

Natural objects are conductors of divinity. They're alive with spirit, power, and wisdom. Cast this spell and discover the gifts and the magic waiting for you in the natural world.

You'll need

~   Your journal and a pen

~   A walk in Nature

Cast your spell

1. Go outside, take a walk in Nature.

2. Allow yourself to be drawn to a natural object that calls or appeals to you. Alternatively, select a natural object that you've already collected. Your home may already be filled with signs of your Witchiness—bowls of stones or shells, jars of feathers or seeds. You may wish to choose one that represents an element you wish to work with.

3. Whatever your object, approach it slowly and with respect. Hold it, feel its weight and texture. Look at it closely, study its structure, observe its color, its nuances. Consider its role in the place where it resides.

4. Ask it to teach you. Listen to what it teaches you about itself, about its world, its role, and the wisdom it embodies.

5. What does it have to teach you about yourself? What blessing does it offer you?

6. Ask the object if it has a name or title. If not, you might like to offer it one. For example, some titles for a pine cone might be: "Seed of Hope and Life Reborn," "Child of Mother Earth," "Dreaming Tree," or "Unfolding Beauty."

7. Write down the wisdom and blessings that have been revealed to you.

8. Ask the object if it is willing to return to your home to work with you as a power object, and if it agrees, thank it and leave something in exchange.

9. You now have an ally, an object of power from which to learn magic and with which to make magic.

Act in accord

Keep your object of power in a place of honor and work with it regularly to deepen your relationship.

From time to time, take it back to where you found each other, so it can recharge.

Spell to Meet the Spirit of the Land

Wherever you live, surrounded by woods or fields, suburban tracts or city skyscrapers, spirits of the land live with you. It can be hard to see what's right in front of you, but the spirit of the land, the *genius loci*, sees you. Cast this spell to remember where you are and what you need to know, what the land needs you to know. There's work to do, and there's wonder to experience.

You'll need

~ To get outside, where you can take off your shoes

~ An offering

Cast your spell

1. Go outside, taking an offering with you, and walk slowly through a garden, field, wood, or park.

2. Take your shoes off. Feel the ground beneath your feet.

3. Look carefully all around you. You are entering liminal space, a place where the worlds of Spirit and Earth meet.

4. Sit down. Close your eyes and ground yourself. Feel the energies flowing through you, around you. Feel your awareness opening into the space around you.

5. Ask the Spirit of the Land, of the place, to visit you. Allow yourself to see, with your eyes closed or open.

6. The Spirit may appear as an animal or plant, a mythic being or a person.

7. Ask what it needs and agree to do what it asks.

8. Thank it for visiting with you and leave your offering.

9. Your spell is cast.

Act in accord

Honor the relationship you have begun with the spirit of the place. Do what was asked of you and continue to visit the spirit and to heal as you take care of each other.

Honeybee Spell

The honeybee is a magical being; honeybee hives are that magic magnified. Traveling between the worlds, bees bless us with the sweetness, healing, and magical powers of the honey they make, their figure-of-eight waggle dances, the hexagonal honeycombs they create. They are guides to the divine garden within us. Cast this honeybee spell and enjoy the sweetness their magic offers.

Cast your spell outside in the Spring, the season of returning bees, but do it anytime you need the sweetness of life.

You'll need

~   A jar of raw local honey

~   A spoon

~   A plate, if indoors

Cast your spell

1.   Purify yourself, and your space if indoors

2.   Place the honey, spoon (and plate) before you.

3.   Feel your desire for sweetness, for love, for healing, for magic in the center of your being, in your heart.

4.   Call the honeybee, call the ancient priestesses of the honeybee, the Melissae, call the Goddess of the Bees.

5. Make the sound of buzzing bees.

6. Walk in a figure of eight, with its point of intersection crossing over the honey.

7. Reach out your arms as if in flight as you do this "waggle dance."

8. If you're outside, pay attention to any visits from honeybees.

9. When your energy has reached its zenith, drop down in front of the honey.

10. Pour some of the honey in the shape of a hexagram on the ground or the plate.

11. Taste the honey. Taste the healing sweetness of life. Taste the love that life offers you. Taste the magic and the blessing of the bees.

12. Thank the bees, thank those who tend them, thank the flowers and Mother Earth.

13. Your spell is cast.

Act in accord

Take or leave the plate outside as an offering to Mother Nature.

Pay attention to the presence of bees in your dreams and your garden.

Consider how to bring more sweetness into your life.

Give back to the bees whose lives are endangered and without whom you cannot live.

Mother Earth's Healing Heartbeat Spell

Mother Earth is suffering and her children are dying because we've forgotten to be grateful. We take without giving back. We've forgotten her wisdom and holy magic too. Cast this spell for Mother Earth and you'll begin to remember who you are: One of her beloved children; where you are: With your Mother and her other children; and why you're here: To *be* the healing change you wish to see in the world and *with* the world.

You'll need

~ Some of a dried medicine plant like yarrow, echinacea, or chamomile

Cast your spell

1. Take your medicine plant and honey and head to a spot of natural peace that calls to you. Sit on Mother Earth. Feel her beneath you, supporting you.

2. Place your left hand on the breast of Mother Earth. Feel the textures of the soil, the grass, the moss. Feel her warmth, her strength, her stability. Thank Mother Earth for her countless blessings, for how she nourishes and sustains your body *and* soul.

3. Breathe. Ground yourself. Feel the energy of Mother Earth filling and nourishing you.

4. Place your right hand on your heart. With your left hand, your heart hand, gently tap the rhythm of your heartbeat: *Bum bump pause, bum bump pause…* Feel your heart's rhythm come into sync with Mother Earth's heart.

5. Feel *your* love and energy flowing into *her*. Send energy to her to help her heal and renew herself. Take your time. Feel the healing power of your connection to each other.

6. Ask her what she needs from you. Listen carefully for her reply. She will tell you or show you.

7. Tell her you will do as she has asked. *Make a promise and mean it.*

8. Thank her for all that she gives you.

9. Leave your medicine plant for her.

10. Your spell is cast.

Act in accord

Keep your promise and do whatever Mother Earth has asked of you.

Pay attention to how you treat Mother Earth every day, and remember to take no more than you need and give back with thanks for what she gives you.

Herne's Talisman for Wild Wisdom (A God Spell)

There's wild magic inside you, an instinct deep within you. Regardless of your gender, it's the untamed animal power of the stag. It's your vitality and sexuality, your drive to succeed and win. These are powerful urges you need in order to be fully alive. Honor the animal part of yourself and you will experience the divinity of your body. Here is a talisman spell for the power of the stag-antlered God of the Wildwood, Herne the Hunter, to help you hunt down and live the life you're meant for.

This is best done in the woods, around dusk when the deer come out to feed in the Fall, but can be done whenever you need it.

You'll need

~ A tablespoon of cedar needles (or 3 drops of cedar oil)

~ A tablespoon of deer's tongue

~ A tablespoon of pine

~ A tablespoon of rue

~ 5 drops of High John the Conqueror essential oil

~ A mortar and pestle

~ A 4-inch (10-cm) square of brown cloth

~ Green or brown cord or ribbon, approximately 6 inches (15 cm) in length

~ A bottle of Water

~ An offering of corn

Cast your spell

1. Be clear in your intention to awaken and respect the wild, instinctual wisdom and strength of your body.

2. Thank the plants for working with you. Grind them together, adding the drops of High John the Conqueror oil.

3. Wrap them in the cloth.

4. Tie the bundle tightly with the cord. Your talisman is ready to be charged.

5. Inhale deeply. Feel a sacred animal power awakening within you.

6. Head to the woods with Herne's talisman, your Water, and your offering.

7. Walk slowly and attentively. Look for deer trails and small trees with buck marking—the bark scraped off by stags rubbing their antlers. If you find one, sit there. Thank the stag for calling you.

8. Press the talisman to the Earth. Ground yourself. Hold the talisman to your heart and begin charging it and yourself.

9. Call Herne:

God of the Wild Wood, Herne the Hunter,
charge and bless this talisman with your wild and holy power.
Charge, strengthen, and empower me.

10. Chant and, if you wish, raise your wild energy by dancing:

   Hoof and horn, hoof and horn, all that dies shall be reborn!

11. Direct your energy into Herne's talisman. When you feel the energy peak, thank Herne, thank Mother Earth, thank the stags. Ground any excess energy into Mother Earth.

12. Drink some Water and offer some to Mother Earth.

13. Sit, listen, pay attention.

14. When you're ready, leave your offering of corn.

15. Your spell is cast.

16. Feel the shift in your body, your energy, your spirit, as you return through the woods. Feel the sharpening of your senses, the pleasure, the power, the magic.

Act in accord

Be prepared to change as Herne guides you in the wild hunt for your embodied Spirit.

Carry the talisman with you until you feel the change is settled in your bones, then return the herbs to where you cast your spell, with thanks to Herne, the stags, and Mother Earth.

Otter Spell for Joy and Harmony

In troubled times it can be hard to feel joy. And yet joy is the very thing that can transform what troubles the world. What you put into the Waters of life goes everywhere throughout Creation, and will be what you take from the Waters of life. Begin with small acts of self-love, kindness, compassion, and patience, and cast this spell to invite Otter to teach you how to play and to fill the Waters of your life, and the life of the world, with joy and love.

You'll need

~ A large enough body of Water to swim in, or a bathtub and bubble bath

Cast your spell

1. Go to the sea, a lake, or a pool, or run a bath and fill it with bubble bath.

2. Call Otter. You'll know when Otter arrives—you'll be smiling.

3. Get into the Water.

4. Float, dive, swim, turn, splash, feel your buoyancy, the coolness of fresh Water, the silliness of bubbles up your nose and between your toes.

5. Play with Otter, diving and spinning and flashing, grabbing your hand in their paw and floating on their back until they get hungry and swim off looking for oysters.

6. Time to get out.

7. Your spell is cast.

Act in accord

Do something fun with a friend.

Be kind, especially to someone whose behavior annoys you.

Feel your joy as others respond to you. You're making the world more joyful with your magic.

Spells for Deep Peace

Though chaos and conflict often seem the sum and total of human civilizations and relations, there are constant and sacred sources of peace to draw from. Here are spells that offer calm, balm and peace for yourself, for those you love and know, for those you don't. Cast these spells and receive the gift of peace, a gift you give the world.

Spell for Peace Within and in the World

The path of the heart is the path of peace, within yourself and in the world. But it's easy for your heart to be troubled when you see the violence and travails humanity creates for itself and for Mother Earth. Take the path into the natural world and let Mother Earth and her other children give you peace. Cast this spell to find the peace within and all around you.

You'll need

~   Nature

Cast your spell

1. Take a walk someplace beautiful and natural.

2. Find a quiet, peaceful, welcoming spot.

3. Center yourself, sit down, breathe, and ground yourself.

4. Feel yourself reconnecting to Creation. Feel the flow of life move through you and back into the world.

5. Look at the beauty, the peace, and life that surround you. The world is full of divine magic. It surrounds you, sustains you, is part of you.

6. Ask Mother Earth for her support as you seek to create peace within yourself and in the world.

7. Read aloud this adaptation of an old Scottish blessing:

Deep peace I breathe into the world.
Deep peace of the blue sky and the soft Air to the world,
deep peace of the shining Sun and the Stars to the world,
deep peace of a soft rain and flowing rivers to the world,
deep peace of the sleeping stones and the green Earth to the world,
deep peace in my heart, deep peace in the world.
Deep peace, deep peace, deep peace.
So mote it be.

8. Rest in the peace within your heart.

9. Thank Mother Earth for the peace she has shared with you. Return home, walking slowly.

10. Your spell is cast.

Act in accord

Carry your peacefulness into the world.

Sigil Spell for Resolving Conflicts and Finding Common Ground

We live in a time of dangerous and exploited divisions—political, racial, ethnic, religious, cultural, economic. But you can make a difference. Cast this spell by creating a magical symbol, a sigil called the *mandorla*, Italian for "almond." It's an ancient symbol of the Mother Goddess, a sacred space and a place of peace where opposites meet to resolve conflicts, overcome divisions, and create shared ground. You can use it to create reconciliation and harmony between yourself and others, or to offer energy to help resolve global conflicts.

September 21, the Autumn (or Spring) Equinox, is the official day of peace, but you can cast this spell anytime it's needed.

You'll need

~   A compass

~   A blue pencil

~   A piece of paper

~   A blue candle

Cast your spell

1. Cast your circle if you wish, and ask for the aid and blessings of the elements, the Sun and Moon and stars above, Mother Earth below, and the Spirit present in the world and in your heart.

2. Ground yourself and draw the energy of Mother Earth into your heart.

3. Light your candle.

4. State your intention:

   I am here to find common ground.
   I am here to create common ground,
   a place of peace where opposites meet.
   I am here to make peace on common ground.

5. Create a *mandorla* to bind back together what has been torn apart:

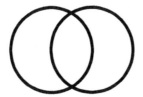

   ▫ Place your compass point on the paper and draw a circle.

   ▫ Mark the center of the circle with a dot.

   ▫ Put the point of the compass on the outside or circumference of the circle and stretch the compass so the pencil reaches the center of the circle.

   ▫ Draw another circle.

   ▫ The oval created by the overlap between the two circles is the *mandorla*, the sign of the Goddess.

6. Within the mandorla, write some words that express your intention, such as:

   Together may we find common ground, peace, understanding,
   the end of conflict, and respect for our differences
   (and whatever else expresses the healing of divisions for you).

7. Where the circles overlap, you have created unity. You have created safety and connection in our fractured world. You have created a sacred space, a place of peace, where opposites are joined together.

8. Place your hands on your *mandorla*. Feel the energies of patience and peace, connection and common ground, empathy and optimism flowing through you.

9. When you're ready, set your spell with these words:

   And so it is, and so it shall be, one by one, beginning with me.

10. Blow out your candle.

11. Your spell is cast.

Act in accord

Keep your *mandorla* where you can see it and draw on its power.

Embody what you seek and the spell will work in the world through you. Begin close to home with a friend, a family member, a neighbor whose views you don't share.

Next time you meet someone with whom you disagree, listen without arguing, seek common ground where you can agree, and respect your differences.

Breaking Bread Spell to Heal Divisions

We cannot live happily or well by treating strangers, neighbors, even family members as enemies, or by being treated as their enemies. How do we heal the divide? Food can bring us together—there's no room for enemies in the kitchen. When you share a meal with someone, you focus on the person, not their politics or their religion, their race or their gender. Change a few people from strangers or "enemies" into friends, and the world begins to change. Cast this kitchen witchery spell to heal divisions by breaking bread.

You'll need

~ To choose something you love to cook

~ People to break bread with

Preparation

~ Gather the ingredients.

Cast your spell

1. Set your intention to bring people together with a good meal.

2. Invite those you love and those you don't, those you know and those you no longer know, old friends and new, a neighbor who is different from you, whatever "different" means. Invite them to break bread with you.

3. Tell them to arrive at a time when you're cooking.

4. Ask them to bring the salad, the dessert, the wine, the bread.

5. Gather them in the kitchen as you work.

6. Have them stir the pot, tear the lettuce, slice the tomatoes, put the dessert on your best serving plate, uncork the wine, take down the glasses, help set the table.

7. When everything is ready, call everyone to the table.

8. Thank them for breaking bread with you.

9. Break the bread and pass it around.

10. Pass the food around.

11. Eat together.

12. Have your guests help you clean up.

13. Your spell is cast and the world is a better place for it.

Random Acts of Kindness Spell

A small, simple act of kindness, random or reciprocal, is its own spell. Kindness benefits the one who receives it and the one who gives it and makes the world a better place for all. This is a spell for creating caring relationships not just with humans, but with all beings, with Mother Earth, and with the spirits that watch over us.

Be kind to yourself, especially if you're someone who always puts others first, neglects your own self-care, and toughs it out—you need kindness too. Cast the spell of kindness and feel yourself change. Feel the world change. It's becoming kinder.

You'll need

~   To be kind

Cast your spell

1. Pick one or more of the following acts of kindness and follow through:

    ▫   Connect with a living being in your neighborhood who might be lonely or in need. It could be a bird, a stray cat, a neighbor, a plant, or yourself. Offer a small act of kindness, support, and compassion.

▢ Visit an area of land that is neglected, damaged, or in need. Connect with the spirit of the wounded place and ask what it needs. Listen for the answer, look for a sign. Do what is asked of you.

▢ Check in on a friend, someone elderly, or someone in need, including yourself. Offer your help, donate your time, write them a note.

▢ Share something with someone—even yourself. Give them/ yourself time, attention, something you've cooked or baked, a note, a favorite book, a small thoughtful gift.

2. Choose a cause you care about, find a group of like-minded people who want to make a difference, and volunteer.

3. Your spell of making the world a kinder place is cast.

Act in accord

Be kind to yourself, to all you encounter, to Mother Earth.

Spells for Wonder

The Mystery is hiding in plain sight. Cast these
spells and remove your blindfold. See the magic of
Creation, the embodiment of Spirit all around and
within you. Feel the wonder as it flows through you,
re-enchanting your life as you re-enchant the world.

Gratitude Spell
for Life's Magic

Give thanks and the world is full of magic. The root of "gratitude" is *gwere*, from the same ancient language that gave us *wicce*; it means "to praise, to celebrate; to be in contact with the Divine." Gratitude is a spell that opens your heart to a sacred world.

Cast this spell and bring wonder into your life. It can be done anywhere, anytime. Outside is wonderful, but the bathroom sink, the kitchen counter, or your desk are fine.

You'll need

~   A small offering

Cast your spell

1. Take a few deep breaths. Be present in this moment.

2. Offer your thanks. Begin with the Prayer Spell below, then when you're ready, write your own:

> *Welcome, Spirit. Welcome, all beings of Creation.*
> *Mother Earth, Father Sun, Sister Moon,*
> *Shining Stars, thank you.*
> *Air and the winds that blow, Fire that burns,*
> *Waters that flow, Earth that nourishes all, thank you.*

Plants, animals, all living beings and spirits,
thank you for your healing, your teaching, your generosity.
Ancestors, thank you for my life and the lessons you offer me.
Teachers, known and yet to come,
thank you for showing me how to live well.
Thank you for giving me all that I need to be healthy
and happy and able to live in harmony.
Thank you for the love that is all around me and within me.
Let me give back in kind for all that I have been given.
Thank you for this life, in this body, in this time and place.
Thank you.
My spell is cast.

3. Rest in the feeling of connection, gratitude, and peace.

Act in accord

Take your feelings of connection, peace, and gratitude into your day.

Breath of Life Spell

This spell works with wisdom given to me by the trees in my garden, who brought me out of a long sorrow. They shared the breath of life with me and brought my spirit back to life and my life back to the world. Everything is breathing together—fish with kelp, bears with pine trees, you with the oak tree in your backyard, humans with the Amazon. When we breathe together, we create the Air that is the breath of life for all living things. We experience the calm, connection, and communion of Creation. Breathe this spell and make magic with the trees and all the Plant People.

This spell is best done outside, sitting on the ground beneath a tree when there are leaves on the trees, but you can do it anywhere, anytime, even in a prison cell. If you're indoors, sit in front of houseplant or close your eyes and visualize a tree you know and love.

You'll need

~ A tree that's willing to work with you

~ Birdseed

~ Some Water

Cast your spell

1. Go for a walk someplace natural that has trees. If you have a tree you work with, go there. Otherwise, find a tree that's willing to work with you. Place your hands on its trunk. Slow yourself down, connect with it, and thank it.

2. Sit down at its roots, lean back, and look up at its immense beauty.

3. Breathe. Inhale for a count of three, hold for two, and exhale for a count of five.

4. Keep breathing until your mind becomes quiet, your body calm. If your mind wanders, just bring it back to your breathing.

5. When you're ready, inhale and bring your attention to receiving the oxygen created for you by the tree. Feel your heart fill with wonder and gratitude.

6. Exhale. Bring your attention to giving the carbon dioxide you create to the tree.

7. Inhale and receive the breath of life, exhale and return the breath of life.

8. Breathe with the tree. Breathe together.

9. Feel the love, gratitude, and breath of life flowing back and forth between you, connecting you. Feel your shared joy.

10. There is no waste. There is only Nature's magic, the breath of life flowing between you and the tree, you and the Plant People.

11. The Divine is a breath away. Breathe gratitude. Breathe love. Breathe.

12. When you are ready, thank the tree. Offer Water and birdseed.

13. Walk home slowly.

Act in accord

Whenever you feel lonely, worried, or disconnected, breathe and remember that wherever you are, you're always connected to the trees, and all the plants, who are breathing with you.

Offering Spell for Mother Earth

With this spell you give back to Mother Earth for all the blessings she has given you.

You'll need

~   A stone

~   Offerings of milk and honey

Cast your spell

1. Find a place outside, in your garden or elsewhere, that you can return to and tend.

2. Greet Mother Earth and place your stone softly at your feet.

3. Sit down. Ground yourself if you wish.

4. Pour the milk and honey onto the stone, letting it spill over onto Mother Earth.

5. Thank her for the blessings she gives you and all beings.

6. Name those blessings. Speak from your heart.

7. Sit quietly and know that Mother Earth's love is everywhere. Offer her your love.

8. Your spell is cast.

Act in accord

Return to Mother Earth and tend her with love.

Drawing Down the Moon (A Goddess Spell)

One of the most sublime and mysterious spells is Drawing Down the Moon, an ancient practice to fill yourself with the radiant power of the Full Moon and the magic of the Goddess. For a brief while, She can see with your eyes and speak with your lips. When She departs, She leaves you transformed.

Cast when the Moon is Full, where its light can shine on you, preferably outdoors in a peaceful and private place.

You'll need

~ A white sheet

~ A bowl of Water if you wish to charge it

~ Something grounding to eat and Water to drink

Preparation

~ Purify yourself first by drinking Water, bathing, or showering.

Cast your spell

1. Cast your circle.

2. Place the bowl of Water in the moonlight to charge.

3. Stand in the moonlight.

4. Wrap yourself in the white sheet. Breathe. Ground yourself.

5. Call the Goddess of the Full Moon to bless you:

> *By bud and flower and fruit, I call upon you,*
> *ancient Goddess of the Full and shining Moon.*
> *Fill me with your presence, bless me with your magic.*

6. Look up at the brilliant Moon, repeating the incantation softly until you feel yourself opening to the presence of the Goddess.

7. Open your arms, spreading the sheet like the wings of the Goddess Isis to capture the magic.

8. Feel the Goddess's presence, energy, and blessings flow into you.

9. When you feel Her presence wane, cross your arms over your heart, wrapping the Moon-charged sheet around you.

10. Pour some Water onto Mother Earth as an offering. Thank the Goddess for blessing you.

11. Be sure to ground any excess energy into Mother Earth.

12. Eat and drink something. Take your time to be in your body.

13. Your spell is cast.

14. Close your circle.

Act in accord

Write about what you experienced and any messages you received.

You may sleep beneath the Moon-charged sheet for prophetic dreams, or fold it carefully and keep it to wear and charge yourself with the Moon's power as you cast your spells. Pour the Moon-Charged Water into a small bottle for future spells.

Spell for
a Prophetic Dream

Each night you close your eyes and enter a realm of magic. You dream. Guides appear and spirits greet you. You grow wings and fly, fur covers you, you swim with seals to the bottom of the sea. Dream and you live between the worlds where the worlds are one. Time disappears and the future appears to reveal your destiny. Cast this spell and let your dreams guide you.

This spell is best done during the Dark Moon at bedtime.

You'll need

~ The ingredients for an old Prophetic Dreaming Potion:

   ▫ Lavender or lavender essential oil

   ▫ Marjoram

   ▫ Mugwort

~ A small muslin bag or cotton handkerchief

~ A mortar and pestle

~ A cup of chamomile tea

~ Your bed

~ Your journal and a pen

Preparation

~ Ask the plants to work with you and thank them for granting you the gift of psychic dreaming.

~ Spoon small amounts of the herbs into the mortar. Grind clockwise, adding small amounts of herbs and oil until the potion has a pleasing aroma.

~ Inhale the magic.

~ Fill the muslin bag with your dream potion or tie it in the cotton handkerchief.

~ Breathe your intention into your Dream Potion.

~ Place it under your pillow.

~ Put your journal and pen by your bed.

Cast your spell

1. Get into bed and drink a cup of chamomile tea. Read something you love, listen to restful music, breathe. Snuggle into your bed and sleep.

2. When you wake up, especially in the middle of the night and before getting out of bed, write down key words about everything you remember from your dreams.

Act in accord

Pay attention to signs or events from your dreams that appear in your waking world.

Dream with your bundle for the next lunar cycle, then return the herbs with gratitude to Mother Earth.

Blessing Spell

A Blessing Spell recognizes holiness and bestows it. Cast a Blessing Spell and the casting will teach you everything you need to know. But before you begin, know that the thing you bless has already blessed you.

Begin by casting a Blessing Spell for yourself. Then bless anything and everyone you like—the swirling snow, the cat curled on the windowsill, the nurse behind her mask, the mailman at your door. Then bless the things or people you don't like.

Watch the magic change you, giving you a heart big enough to bless the world and to receive its blessings. Cast this spell and experience wonder.

You'll need

~ Time

~ Attention

Cast your spell

Cast this spell anytime you're moved to. You may wish to stand before a mirror, outside on Mother Earth, beneath the Moon, up to your ankles in the sea, or sitting at the kitchen table.

1. Take a few calming breaths.

2. Place your hands over your heart and say:

I cast this spell to bless this life I have been given.
Bless my mind with its wonderings and wisdom,
bless my heart with its loves and sorrows,
bless my body with its aches and ecstasies,
bless my spirit with its Fire and its magic.
Bless this day I have been given, with all the beauty
and blessings this world bestows upon me.
I am blessed with wonder and with
gratitude, and so I bless the world.

3. Your Blessing Spell is cast.

Act in accord

Cast your Blessing Spells for yourself and for the world.

Mystery Beyond Understanding Spell

Step into Nature's beauty, its mystery, magnitude, and magic, and experience awe. Witness a murmuration—the spectacle of countless starlings flocking in vast dancing masses across the sky, or schools of flashing fish in the sea, twisting and turning without calamity, coordinating in ways that are a mystery. Cast this spell and experience the wonder beyond understanding.

It's best cast with starlings at dusk between October and March.

You'll need

~ To find a murmuration near you or to make a pilgrimage to find birds or fish, or attend a performance by a favorite performer before a large audience.

Cast your spell

1. Find a murmuration.

2. Approach it slowly, standing where it is easily witnessed—above you in the sky, beneath you in the sea, all around you in the concert hall.

3. Witness the invisible connection made visible, the bliss embodied, the mystery ecstatically revealed.

4. Feel your soul leap with the turning, bending, spinning, ascending, plunging, clapping, swaying individuals moving together, changing direction together, in an instant, in joy.

5. Lift your arms, bend and stretch and move. Give yourself to the energy, the bliss. Feel yourself alive in the presence of magic, participating in a spell cast by Creation.

6. Let your spirit soar in wonder.

7. Your spell is cast.

Act in accord

Pay attention and bear witness to the mystery and the magic.

Spell for Living Well

Your eyes, and your heart, are opening to a world of divine magic that has been with you and in you all along, guiding, supporting, and loving you. Choose any path and it is lit by the stars above you, supported by Mother Earth beneath you, blessed by all the life that surrounds you. Here is a spell crafted from spells as old as time to fill your heart with wonder and to offer the wonder of you to the world. Here is the spell for living well.

You'll need

~   A starry night

Cast your spell

1.   When the night sky is clear, go out and stand beneath the stars.

2.   Make a wish upon the first one you see.

3.   Reach your arms out and spin and dance and feel your power to make your wish come true. Feel the magic.

4.   Feel the divine power of Creation spinning above you, beneath you, through you. Everything is dancing. Dance until you're breathless.

5.   Now reach up and touch your fingertip to your star. Carry its brilliant light down and into your heart. Close your hands over your heart.

6.   Chant the Spell for Living Well:

> *I am starlight shining in the world as I walk.*
> *I am chanting the spell of living well.*
> *I am ancient dust and Water walking,*
> *I am chanting the spell of living well…*

7. Continue chanting. Feel the magic working within you.

8. Chant until the magic reaches the furthest stars above you. You are Life embodying Spirit. You are the love spell cast by Creation. You are magic.

9. When you're ready, thank the stars that light the path before you—into yourself and into the world. Thank Mother Earth for giving life to Spirit and to you.

10. Go inside, drink some Water, go to bed, and when you wake up, live well.

11. Your spell is cast…

Act in accord

Manifest your magic. Carry your starlight, your love and wonder, into the world and live well.

My Returning Home
Spell for You

There is a reason that you are here, now—a sense of purpose that summons you, a call that's stirred your spirit, a spell that's awakened you. And so, before we ring the bell, close the book, and blow out the candle, I offer you this blessing spell, from my heart to yours, for your wondrous journey home to a world of holy magic that's awaiting your return.

Cast your spell

1. Stand, setting your feet slightly apart, firmly but softly upon our Mother Earth.

2. Place your hands over your heart and feel it beating.

3. Breathe and feel life flowing through you.

4. Feel your heart grow larger.

5. Open out your arms.

6. Feel your heart opening to Creation.

7. Feel the heart of Creation opening to you.

8. Listen to the song of Creation being sung all around you.

9. Bring your hands to your heart and receive this blessing spell. (You may wish to say it aloud and say "me" instead of "you," "my" instead of "your.")

May Spirit and World be One within you.
May your heart be open to the Life that
welcomes you into its heart.
May the magic of love flow into you and
through you into the world.
May your life be blessed and may the Life
of the world be blessed by you.
So mote it be.

10. Our spell is cast. Our circle is open but never broken.

Life in Accord

You are alive at a critical moment. For centuries, we have dis-enchanted the world, sending the Sacred so far away that the Divine seems to have died. The consequences are dire—the future of life hangs in the balance. Mother Earth is calling us home, calling us to help life flourish in health, harmony, and love.

Writing is an enchantment; these spells are my offering to help you awaken the divine magic within you and all around you. May your heart open into the divine heart of Creation. May your magic shape your purpose, the thing that gives you joy in the doing and that makes the world a better place for your having been here. May you re-enchant your life and the world.

Let us set our spell together and say: "Merry meet, and merry part, and merry meet again!"

I will see you soon.

Correspondences
and Helpful
Information

Table of Correspondences

Direction	East	South
Element	Air	Fire (Earth, Southern Hemisphere)
Nature	wind, breeze	Sun
Aspects	Mind; to know	Will; to dare
Qualities	imagination, intelligence, intuition, communication, poetry, music, language	passion, joy, courage, determination, desire, power, transformation, action, focus
Colors	white, pale blue, lavender	red, orange, yellow
Symbols	feather	candle
Time	dawn	midday
Season	Spring	Summer
Animal	[wing] bird, butterfly, dragonfly	[claw] dragon, lion, lizard
Plant	lavender, bodhi tree	myrrh, olive tree
Tool	athame, sword	wand
Astrological sign	Aquarius, Gemini, Libra	Aries, Leo, Sagittarius
Spirit form	Sylph	Salamander
Goddess	Arianrhod, Aurora, Isis	Ameratsu, Brigid, Pele
God	Hermes, Quetzalcoatl, Thoth	Horus, Lugh, Sol, Surya

Table of Correspondences

Direction	West	North
Element	Water	Earth (Fire, Southern Hemisphere)
Nature	oceans, rivers, rain, lakes	mountains, woods, fields, caves
Aspects	Heart/womb; to feel	Body; to manifest
Qualities	love, compassion, emotions, dreams, ancestors, reflection, purification, connection	creativity, fertility, rebirth, strength, stability, abundance, generosity, balance
Colors	blue, sea green	green, brown, gold, purple
Symbols	sunset	seed
Time	dusk/twilight	midnight
Season	Autumn	Winter
Animal	[fin] dolphin, fish, otter, whale	[paw, hoof, and horn] bear, bison, horse, stag, wolf
Plant	St John's wort, willow	patchouli, oak
Tool	cauldron, cup	pentacle, stone
Astrological sign	Cancer, Pisces, Scorpio	Capricorn, Taurus, Virgo
Spirit form	Undine	Gnome
Goddess	Aphrodite, Tiamat, Yemaya	Demeter, Freya, Parvati
God	Agwe, Njord, Poseidon	Cernunnos, Dionysus, Green Man, Osiris

Intentions, Herbs, Oils, Minerals

FOR ANXIETY	
Herbs	chamomile, jasmine, lavender, vervain
Oils	frankincense
Minerals	aventurine, hematite

FOR BALANCE	
Herbs	angelica, basil, chamomile, sage, vervain, yarrow
Oils	patchouli, sandalwood
Minerals	amber, tiger's eye, tourmaline (green)

FOR CLEANSING (PURIFICATION)	
Herbs	angelica, basil, chamomile, clove, lavender, sage, St John's wort, yarrow
Oils	myrrh, patchouli
Minerals	fluorite, garnet, tourmaline (black)

FOR COMMUNICATION	
Herbs	blackberry, jasmine, lavender
Oils	allspice
Minerals	blue lace agate, jasper, selenite

FOR COURAGE (CONFIDENCE)	
Herbs	basil, rosemary, yarrow
Oils	allspice, cardamom, frankincense
Minerals	aquamarine, lapis lazuli

FOR DREAMS	
Herbs	angelica, jasmine, lavender, peppermint
Oils	anise, cedar
Minerals	alexandrite, amethyst

FOR ENERGY	
Herbs	basil, carnation, cinnamon, nutmeg, peppermint, rose, sage, St John's wort
Oils	allspice, dragon's blood, star anise
Minerals	Apache tears, bloodstone, jasper (red)

FOR GROUNDING	
Herbs	blackberry, chamomile, sage, vervain
Oils	myrrh, patchouli, sandalwood
Minerals	hematite, malachite, peridot

FOR HEALING	
Herbs	allspice, angelica, blackberry, chamomile, jasmine, lavender, marjoram, rosemary, rue, yarrow
Oils	dragon's blood, ginger, ginseng, sandalwood
Minerals	blue lace agate, carnelian, citrine, malachite, tourmaline (green, pink)

FOR LOVE	
Herbs	carnation, dill, marjoram, poppy, rose, spearmint
Oils	frankincense, ginger, saffron
Minerals	desert rose, jasper (pink), rose quartz, turquoise

(continued)

FOR MAGIC (PSYCHIC AWARENESS)	
Herbs	basil, dandelion, mint, sage, St John's wort, vervain, yarrow
Oils	cedar, ginger, ginseng, patchouli
Minerals	amber, lodestone, obsidian

FOR PROSPERITY	
Herbs	basil, blackberry, chamomile, dill, marjoram, St John's wort
Oils	ginger, myrrh, saffron
Minerals	aventurine, jade, star sapphire

FOR PROTECTION	
Herbs	angelica, basil, blackberry, dandelion, dill, marjoram, vervain, yarrow
Oils	cedar, spruce, walnut, yew
Minerals	amber, garnet, hematite, rose quartz

FOR RELEASE	
Herbs	basil, clover, fern, foxglove, rosemary, sage, yarrow
Oils	clove, frankincense, patchouli, sandalwood
Minerals	agate, lapis lazuli, malachite

FOR STRENGTH	
Herbs	angelica, basil, comfrey, mint, nutmeg, sage, St John's wort, yarrow
Oils	frankincense, myrrh, vanilla
Minerals	amethyst, hematite, lapis lazuli, moss agate

Colors and Elements

COLOR	ELEMENT	CORRESPONDENT QUALITY
red	Fire	passion, courage, focus
orange	Fire	success, healing, joy
yellow	Fire/Earth	illumination, success, healing
green	Earth	creativity, abundance, growth, rebirth
blue	Water	healing, peace, dreams, womb-resting
indigo	Water/Air	intuition, memory, dreaming, altered states, spirit
purple	Air	intuition, inspiration, divination
pink	Goddess	Divine Feminine, women's mysteries, joy
brown	Earth	Mother Earth, soil, growth, justice, stability, strength
white	Spirit	purification, beginnings, peace, creativity, healing
black	Mystery	the unknown, deep rest, death; absorbs or repels negativity, all colors
silver	Goddess	Divine Feminine, Moon
gold	God	Divine Masculine, Sun

Timing

Timing to Maximize Manifestation

ENERGY	TIME OF DAY	DAYS OF THE WEEK	PHASE OF THE MOON
creativity, beginning	dawn	Sunday, Monday	New Moon
action, attraction	midday	Tuesday, Wednesday	Waxing Moon
abundance, fertility	twilight, dusk	Thursday, Friday	Full Moon
banishing, releasing, reflecting	midnight	Saturday, Sunday	Waning Moon

Timing to Maximize Manifestation Continued

ENERGY	SEASON OF THE YEAR	SABBATS	ELEMENTS
creativity, beginning	Spring	Imbolc, Ostara	Air
action, attraction	Summer	Beltaine, Summer Solstice	Fire
abundance, fertility	Autumn	Lughnasadh, Mabon	Water
banishing, releasing, reflecting	Winter	Samhain, Winter Solstice	Earth

Lunar Phases, Energies, and Timing

Time your spells in sync with the right phase of the Moon and the Moon's magic will increase their potency and likelihood of success.

New Moon

(from the end of Waning, no visible Moon)

Spells for divination, for liminality, to honor mysteries, wisdom, seeing the unseen, putting a stone on it (ending).

Waxing Moon

(from New until Full)

Spells for setting intentions and goals, planning, new beginnings, new projects, new good habits, self-care, well-being, rejuvenation, personal improvement, growth and increase, healing, prosperity.

Full Moon

(one to three days)

Spells for fulfillment, manifestation, abundance, love, wealth, creativity, well-being, and good health.

Waning Moon

(from Full until Dark)

Banishing, releasing, removing, ending, breaking bad habits, addictions, negativity, getting rid of debt and bad health.

Seasonal Sabbats, Energies, and Timing

Samhain

October 31, Northern Hemisphere; May 1, Southern Hemisphere

Let go of the past; honor what's ending; rest in emptiness between past and future; enter the Dreamtime. Let go, be.

Winter Solstice

December 21, Northern Hemisphere; June 21, Southern Hemisphere

Find the light within the darkness; a light is shining within you, enough to see the future; honor your dream of what comes next. Seek inspiration.

Imbolc

February 1, Northern Hemisphere; August 1, Southern Hemisphere

Find joy in small things; life is stirring in the belly of the world and in you. Have hope.

Spring Equinox

March 21, Northern Hemisphere; September 21, Southern Hemisphere

Mother Earth is returning to life and so should you; feel yourself awakening and tend to your goals; rest in between past and future; light and life are returning. Rebirth!

Beltaine

May 1, Northern Hemisphere; October 31, Southern Hemisphere

Celebrate! Nature is alive and beautiful and so are you! Honor your body, its desires and wisdom. Love.

Summer Solstice

June 21, Northern Hemisphere; December 21, Southern Hemisphere

The Sun is at its zenith and the Earth is responding; feel the surging energies of life; work toward your goals; everything is growing and so are you. Prosperity.

Lughnasadh

August 1, Northern Hemisphere; February 1, Southern Hemisphere

Take a rest and enjoy the fruits of your hard work; change is manifesting; the light is lessening, but Mother Earth's bounty is increasing. Gratitude.

Autumn Equinox

September 21, Northern Hemisphere; March 21, Southern Hemisphere

Honor the abundance of Mother Earth; honor and harvest what you've accomplished; discern the lessons of all the challenges you've faced and find the seed of what comes next. Rest in between past and future; the dark Dreamtime is coming. Discernment.

Acknowledgments

Every book requires circles of love and care to arrive in the world. My deep thanks to Michelle Pilley, publisher and managing director of Hay House UK, for her continuing creative, wise, and visionary support, art director Leanne Siu Anastasi for her inspired design, and dear friend and artist Danielle Barlow for the spellcasting cover and interior art. My heartfelt thanks continues to Susie Bertinshaw, Julie Oughton, Lizzi Marshall, Portia Chauhan, Lizzie Henry, Alexandra Gruebler, and the rest of the HH family who've brought their expertise, enthusiasm, and bright spirits to midwife this magical offering to the world. My deep gratitude to the many foreign publishers for bringing *Spells for Living Well* to readers around the globe, and to my agent, Cullen Stanley, for her confidence in my certainty that the world needs her Witches.

This creation was blessed by my loving, funny, smart circle of sacred magic makers, adventurers, and dear friends—my knight, Christopher Fielding, with his stalwart devotion and daily magic, wise and wonderful messaging magician Heather Vee, Emily Fitz for invaluable professional therapist's input on the self-care spells, Angelica Chayes for the Sleep Well Potion and world-changing strategizing, Pat Fero for her nourishing support, Cora van Leeuwen and Autumn Reed for tending our Awaken the Witch Within community, and Juliet Weber, Noreen, Dave, and Jeannine for their precious, patient, generous friendships.

My wonderful, international Patreon community, especially our monthly Crafters Circle, and the countless readers, students, practitioners, fans, seekers, and Witches around the world with whom I work have inspired this lastest effort to guide our paths home—thank you for your passion, curiosity, and wonder. My gratitude includes dear friends and supporting institutions over the last few years of innovating work: Twila York and the Greater Chicago Pagan Pride, Rev. Diane Berke and Ilene Sameth and One Spirit Learning Alliance, John Cianciosi and the Theosophical Society in America, Prof. Mara Keller and the California Institute of Integral Studies, *Kindred Spirit*, and all the friends and colleagues who so generously provided endorsements and aid in getting news of this magical collection of enchantments to the world.

I am blessed and sustained by the inner and ever-expanding circles that have inspired and worked with me for the 40 years of magic from which *Spells for Living Well* was drawn; together we've created and grown the Tradition of Ara, the Temple of Ara, the Tempio di Ara. Thank you for your love, courage, and devotion,

Priestesses and Priests, *primer inter pares* Linda Maglionico, Ally Machate, Kirsten Rostedt, Valeria Trisolglio, Amalia Dellaquila, Dario Pastore, Giula Turolla, Charlie, Cory, Lorenza M., Margaret, Melody, Barbara, Patty, Tina, Alissa, Kenwyn, whose memory is a blessing, Dr. Eileen, Andreas, Mena, Amy, Heather, and all the remarkable initiates, clergy in training, and devotees around the world.

At the center of the circle of my life, my husband, Phil Loria, is proof that love is the greatest magic, and of course Foxie. You keep my heart filled with gratitude.

Deep thanks to you who hold this book in your hands and who will cast the spells to make your life and the world a better place.

Deep thanks to those who came before and who left their magic for those of us who follow.

Deep thanks for Mother Earth and all her children, for the spirits of place, the spirits of Creation, the spirits of the peoples on whose land I now live, for teaching me.

Deep thanks for the Mystery hiding in plain sight. May I continue to seek, to see, and to serve my purpose, and may it continue to give me strength to help make the world a better place for all Life. Deep thanks.

About the Author

Photo credit: David Benthal

Phyllis Curott is one of America's first public Witches, the world's most widely published and internationally bestselling Wiccan author, an attorney whose groundbreaking cases secured the legal rights of Witches, and an interfaith activist who has helped make Witchcraft the fastest-growing spirituality in America.

The recipient of numerous honors, Phyllis was named one of the Ten Gutsiest Women of the Year by *Jane* magazine and inducted into the Martin Luther King, Jr. Collegium of Clergy and Scholars. *New York* magazine has called her teaching the culture's "next big idea" and *Time* magazine published her as one of "America's leading thinkers." Her YouTube series on Wicca has almost 3 million views and her *Awaken the Witch Within* course is available online. Founder of the Temple of Ara, Phyllis is a Trustee of the Parliament of the World's Religions and is the Program Chair for the 2023 Parliament.

Phyllis continues to write, provide personal consultations, mentoring, and readings, teach, and lecture internationally on Nature's sacred magic and why the world needs her Witches.

www.phylliscurott.com

phylliscurott

@phylliscurott

@phylliscurott

PhyllisCurottWitchcrafting

Find Phyllis's *Awaken the Witch Within* online course at:
www.hayhouseu.com/awaken-the-witch-within-online-course-hhu

And Phyllis's membership at:
www.patreon.com/phylliscurott